...BUT I HAVEN'T GOT TIME TO COOK!

Northern College of Acupuncture

This book was kindly donated by
Sonia Williams

WITHDRAWN

by
Liz Thearle Dip ION

©2002 Liz Thearle

First published in 2002 by
Printing Matters
The Coach House
Burford House Gardens
Tenbury Wells
Worcestershire
WR15 8HQ

The moral rights of the author have been asserted

ISBN 0 9544134 0 7

Designed and set by Jennie Braithwaite

Printed and bound in Great Britain

Contents

Forward   5

Acknowledgements   6

Introduction   7

1. **A Word on Organics**   9
   The importance of eating organically produced food

2. **Stocking the store-cupboard;**   13
   feeding the freezer
   The importance of advance planning

3. **Fabulous Fats**   19
   Using the right fats and oils
   - dangers of the fat-free diet

4. **Dealing with Diets**   23
   - a word on wheat
   - doubts about dairy
   - sugar-free

5. **Going Nuts? Running to Seed?**   43
   Including nuts and seeds in your diet

6. **Treat yourself to Tofu**   59
   Why we need it and how to overcome our natural reluctance to use it.

7. **The Big Breakfast**   69
   Philosophy; menus and recipes

CONTENTS

8. Squeezing the Last Ounce   77
Juicing for health

9. The Portable Lunch   83
Not a sarnie in sight

10. Slow, Slow, Quick, Quick, Slow   91
Slow cooker techniques for ready-when-you-get-home meals

11. Under Pressure   107
Pressure cooking. Methods and recipes.

12. Feeding the Family   121
Getting children away from pizza and fish fingers
- teaching them that cooking can be fun.

13. Satisfying Stirfries   139
Quick and nutritious meals in one (large) pan

14. Meal in a Soup   143
More one-pan cooking

15. Snacks   155
Healthy alternatives to biscuits, crisps and chocolate

16. Dressing for Dinner   159
Sauces and dressings

17. The 30-minute Dinner Party   171
Preparing in advance - quick and impressive dishes

List of Recipes   188

Forward

Most of us are digging our own graves with a knife and fork. When the penny drops and you realise that its time to change your diet, whether inspired by a health problem or the shere logic of the 'optimum nutrition' approach, now backed by decades of good science, the question is how? What do you buy? How do you prepare it? What do you eat?

Liz Thearle has done a tremendous job helping you put optimum nutrition principles into practice. This book gives you all the straight forward, practical, hands-on information you need to change your diet in a positive way. You'll find so many pearls of wisdom, and delicious recipes, to make the practice of optimum nutrition effortless and enjoyable. The rewards of eating, and living in this way are many. Better energy, less infections, improved skin and, in short, a longer and healthier life.

Wishing you good luck, good health and bon appetit!

Patrick Holford

Founder of the Institute for Optimum Nutrition

Acknowledgements

Every time I have heard a negative comment about food and cooking from my clients, I have wished that there was a book which would give them the information they need to change their attitude to food. Every time someone asks me how to use a particular, suggested ingredient, I have wished that I could recommend just one book, instead of using up valuable consultation time giving sample recipes and methods of cooking.

I could not, however, have written this book without help from other people. Sue Rose my oldest (long term!) friend whose support and experience of writing a cookery column have been invaluable.

Jennie Braithwaite, my Editor, has been just fantastic, working long hours on the design and layout of the book, while retaining her cool and sense of humour.

Thanks to Morphy Richards for donating a Slow Cooker to replace my aging one, and to Tefal for an X-Press Cooker and demonstrating that it is no longer something to be feared. Also to Berrydales Publishers and to Mother Hemp for some innovative recipes.

Shortly before going to press, I heard an excellent talk by Linda Brown, the food writer and consumer champion, at Penrhos Court, Kington, Herefordshire. Although a firm believer in organic produce, I could not have put the case quite as well as she did - thank you Linda.

Finally, I would like to thank Patrick Holford who has taught me much of what I know about the benefits of good nutrition and healthy eating, and who has given his support to this book.

INTRODUCTION

This book is written for everyone who knows that they would benefit from eating healthily but either feels that they simply don't have the time or are confused by the various messages they are receiving as to what is and what is not "healthy". It is equally valid for the career-orientated workaholic and the working mother (or father) as it is for the person who lives alone and feels that it is just too much effort to cook for one. It aims to simplify the incorporation of foods which we are told we should be eating, but haven't a clue what to do with them.

Above all, it aims to give quick and easy recipes - and methods of cooking - for the type of food which will make you feel good, look good and improve your energy levels. It is for carnivores, vegetarians and vegans; for young and old; and for those who are struggling to adapt their diet in order to avoid foods to which they are allergic or intolerant. Each recipe contains a limited number of ingredients rather than a long, off-putting list, and should take only about 20 minutes to prepare.

It is about learning to enjoy food instead of regarding it as a chore to prepare or something which makes you fat. It includes a chapter on snacks (healthy ones!) the downfall of so many of us.

LIZ THEARLE is a qualified Nutritional Therapist who trained at the Institute for Optimum Nutrition in London. She has been practising in Hereford and London for 15 years, and is a member of the British Association of Nutritional Therapists. Above all, however, she loves good food and, however punishing the schedule, is simply not prepared to compromise by grabbing an unhealthy snack or, even worse, skipping a meal.

Over the years, Liz has seen many people literally transform their lives and their energy levels through a change in diet. This is not surprising when we consider that over 80% of ill-health can be either directly or indirectly attributed to poor diet. Irritable bowel syndrome, arthritis, eczema and asthma, to name but a few, are reaching epidemic levels and most cases can be alleviated by an improved diet. Nor are the benefits confined to physical well-being mood swings, irritability and hyperactivity in children are also strongly influenced by what we eat.

This book is her philosophy on how to spend the minimum time gaining maximum benefit (and enjoyment!) from every-day food.

SUE ROSE is a busy public relations consultant and former cookery columnist who also believes passionately in the benefits of good food. In spite of her busy schedule she frequently entertains and appears to produce a delicious three-course meal with the minimum of effort; often within an hour of arriving home from work.

Liz and Sue are both avowed "foodies" and friends since schooldays. Ideas and recipes are taken from their very varied experience of shopping, preparing and cooking food, both in England and on their travels around the world, experimenting with local produce.

They hope that this book will give you an abundance of ideas on "Healthy Eating in a Hurry" and that it will inspire you to cook each and every day without it seeming to be a chore.

A Word On Organics

1

I am often asked if it is really worth paying the extra for organically produced food. Quite apart from the fact that the flavour is usually so much better, it tends to have a higher content of the trace elements which are essential to good health.

Buying organic vegetables can actually save shopping time, as organic box schemes have tended to proliferate over the last few years. These are delivered to your home on a weekly basis, and are run by organic growers. A full list can be found in the Soil Association book *Where to Buy Organic Food*. There are also various retailers around the country who stock organic foods, and these are listed in the *Organic Directory* published by Green Books in conjunction with the Soil Association. The Internet is also a good source of suppliers.

Unfortunately, about two-thirds of all organic produce sold through supermarkets is imported, and the nutritional value of such produce is considerably lower than the equivalent product which is grown locally. In addition, there is the high cost to the environment of transporting food around the world.

At a recent seminar on "Our Food Heritage" held in June 2002 at Penrhos Court, Kington in Herefordshire, Lynda Brown made the following points:

"We deserve pure, nutritious food that we can trust. It is our birthright! We did not evolve to cope with colourings, flavourings, pesticides and other additives. No wonder we suffer increasingly from conditions such as eczema and asthma, and our children are hyperactive. Nor were we designed to eat what is known as "mechanically recovered meat" - the bits you really don't want to know about, which are turned into slurry and consumed by the truckload.

The only foods you can really trust these days are those you grow or raise yourself (a real luxury!),certified organic produce, or food which comes from small, local, caring producers. You can buy such food in farm shops and farmers' markets, where you will probably meet the people who produced it and who will be pleased to tell you how and where it was produced.

The Benefits of Organic Food

1. Field to plate traceability

2. Must be produced in ways which protect the environment

3. Better animal welfare (even if you don't eat meat, cows are reared in unnatural conditions to produce milk and cheese; chickens are raised to produce excessive amounts of eggs. If we had farmed organically, we would not have had Foot and Mouth Disease.

4. Free from Genetic Modification.

5. Absence of pesticide residues - did you know that the average daily diet to-day contains over 30 different pesticides? Animals are fed antibiotics, growth hormones, and foods which they would never eat in their natural habitat. With organic foods, there are only seven natural processing aids, instead of a cocktail of 7,000 which are allowed in the conventional food industry.

6. Positive nutritional benefits. Generally speaking, it does contain more vitamins and minerals. Cows fed on grass - and particularly cows reared organically - produced milk with higher levels of linoleic acid, which is essential for the brain.

7. Choice. At present we have a choice about the food we buy. However, unless we radically change our view of food and the critical role it should play in our lives, I don't believe we will have that choice much longer. Then the supermarkets and GM giants will have won!

Many of us believe the myth that we are all too busy to buy and cook real food and at at best, this is done as a weekend hobby. We have lost sight of the fact that food is first and foremost nourishment - not just for the body, but for the mind and soul too.

Research has shown over and over again that, if we want to protect ourselves from the ever-increasing incidence of cancer, we need to increase our consumption of fruit, vegetables, pulses, whole grains and oily fish. Eating organic and locally produced foods will ensure a higher content of the essential, protective nutrients.

Not only do we deserve natural food as our birthright, we also deserve to nourish ourselves. To use the well-known advertising phrase **"we're worth it"**.

With thanks to Lynda Brown, Food writer and consumer champion.

Stocking the store cupboard; Feeding the freezer

2

Are you, like so many people seeking my professional advice on nutrition, just simply too busy to get out a cookery book and make a meal from scratch? If so, then this book is for YOU! It was inspired by two often repeated complaints in my clinic: "But I just don't have time to cook" and "what do I do with these 'healthy' foods you want me to eat?" Foods which people initially have problems incorporating into their diet are, in particular, things like tofu and soya products, and nuts and seeds. People also feel somewhat daunted when I suggest a wheat-, dairy-, or sugar-free diet.

A prerequisite for a new cookery book is that it contains references to "quick and easy" or "superfast" foods as I tend to switch off when I see complicated recipes with lots of ingredients. Such books are no longer confined to every-day use, but have now become the inspiration for lunch, supper or dinner parties, with day-to-day meals being simply a few really good ingredients in imaginative combinations. Even with such simplified recipes, wherever possible, I try to cook sufficient to put a portion or two into the freezer ready for an even more super-fast meal.

Organization

Eating healthily when you lead a busy life is not so much about spending hours looking through recipes, shopping and cooking, but rather it is about **organizing** a supply of healthy and appetizing food - stocking the storecupboard and feeding the freezer. Now this **does** take a little time. It involves sitting down with a book like this and making a **huge** list. It then means taking an hour or two to shop and a little time afterwards dividing your bulk purchases into person/family sized portions for the freezer. This challenging task should, however, only need to be done every three months or so, which most of us can manage if we make it a priority.

Feeding the freezer

From a local supplier, I get beautiful organically reared meat. She also produces good sausages, special "burgers" and bacon, which taste completely different to the supermarket varieties. I tend to buy half a lamb or half a kid at a time, some beef when it is available, and liver which I know is safe to eat. For a similar supplier in your area, contact The Soil Association, tel. 0117 929 0661, or look in your local Green Pages Directory. The Soil Association website is: www.soilassociation.org - look for "organic directory". Alternatively, they produce a pocket sized book for £4.95 + £1.00 postage & packing. Their address is: 40/56 Victoria Street, Bristol BS1 1BY.

Living on my own during the week, I generally package things into single portions. It is then a simple matter of extracting packets from the freezer when they are required. When desperate, the sausages, mince, burgers and bacon can be cooked from frozen, although I do try and organize the day's meals either the night before or in the morning.

A trip to my fishmonger provides a three months' supply of fish. Once again, this is wrapped into suitable portions or, where freezing whole fish such as trout, wrapped separately so that they are easy to take out. Most fishmongers (even those at fish counters in the larger supermarkets) are only too pleased to de-head, fillet and skin the fish so that it is ready to cook. I think most people who are reluctant to cook fish dislike the preparation or the thought of it being full of bones. Some also dislike the smell, which is virtually eradicated if it is cooked in the oven.

Most health food shops will supply large quantities of dried foods at a discount. I am lucky enough to have a supplier locally who sells nuts, seeds, and pulses by the kilo and grains in 5kg packs. I divide the nuts and seeds into half-pound packs and freeze them in order to retain their freshness. Then, as they are needed, I bring a fresh pack into the fridge for everyday use (being full of natural oils, they will go rancid if not refrigerated). Grains, pulses and pasta can be stored in jars for up to a year. Packets of dried fruits, sun-dried tomatoes, mushrooms etc. are very useful for livening up basic foods.

Good quality water is a very important factor in a healthy diet, and my own preference is to have a water filter with its own tap fitted to the kitchen sink. This is supplied by FRESH WATER FILTER (tel: 020 8597 3233 or www.freshwaterfilter.com). Also, it is becoming increasingly easier to have fresh water delivered to your doorstep by companies such as Nature Springs (0800 919805). If you prefer to use a filter jug, refills can be bought in bulk, as can bottles of spring water.

The supermarket, too, can be a source of healthy "convenience" foods, as they now stock an every-increasing range of organic foods. No store cupboard should be without tins of tomatoes, ready-cooked pulses such as kidney, aduki, butter, pinto and black-eyed beans, chick peas and lentils. And what would we do without tins of tuna, salmon, sardines, pilchards, olives, anchovies etc.? Packets of oat cakes, Ryvita and rice cakes make quick fillers, and more and more gluten-free products are now available.

Most of the recipes in this book are wheat and dairy-free as I find that an increasing number of my clients are intolerant of these. If you are, however, able to eat wheat, it is useful to buy good whole-meal bread and rolls by the dozen to keep in the freezer. Rye and spelt bread, as well as pumpernickel slices freeze well. When buying whole loaves, slice them before freezing so that you only need to take out a few slices at a time if required.

Useful standby foods include:

Wholegrain rice	barley	oatflakes
Quinoa	millet	riceflakes
Buckwheat	chick peas	millet flakes
Red and green lentils	puy lentils	a selection of dried beans
Dried apricots	prunes	raisins
Bouillon or stock powder	sun-dried tomatoes	a selection of pasta
Tins or jars of olives	dried mushrooms	Miso
Quorn	tofu	textured soya protein
tinned fruit in its own juice	tinned tomatoes	dried herbs
Curry powders in different strengths		garlic

Seeds - sunflower, pumpkin, linseeds, sesame, hemp

Nuts - almonds, walnuts, hazelnuts, Brazil nuts, cashew nuts

When it comes to fresh fruit and vegetables, this is obviously a little more difficult. The organic box scheme is proliferating over the country and it could be that there is a scheme in operation near you. This varies slightly from place to place, but usually involves ordering a weekly box of, say, £5 or more in value, and collecting it from a central distribution point. Some suppliers also include fruit. For further information on this scheme, contact The Soil Association (see page 15). It is also often possible to buy, say, a tray of apples for storing, a sack of potatoes, or strings of onions and garlic.

EQUIPMENT

I'm not a great fan of gadgets - most of them take far too long to clean in proportion to their usefulness. Two things I would definitely NOT do without, however, are my liquidizer and coffee grinder (for nuts and seeds), which are absolutely essential for so many quick and easy meals and are so inexpensive to buy nowadays. It may sound like a contradiction in terms, but a slow cooker is also high on my list of priorities. A few minutes spent earlier in the day can result in a delicious meal later and it can be very comforting to know that, even if you or one of the family are delayed for an hour or two, the meal will be waiting, unspoiled and smelling delicious, to be taken out and served. An electric steamer with two or three layers is also a convenient and healthy way to prepare a meal.

You may be wondering why we have not included a chapter on micro-wave cooking which would seem to be an obvious method of preparing a quick meal. Quite simply, we are not convinced of its complete safety. A Swiss food scientist, Dr Hans-Ulrich Hertel, discovered in 1989 that there were significant changes in the blood of those who had consumed microwaved food, although he was prohibited by the Swiss Court from claiming that microwave ovens were dangerous to health. The Russians too carried out intensive research into microwave ovens, resulting in their ban in Russia from 1976 until lifting of the ban after Perestroika. Other research done in Britain, Japan and the US has produced similar disquieting results. Quite apart from the unknown safety aspect, microwaved food also tends to be low in flavour. On the other hand, a pressure cooker, or its up-dated version the Express Cooker, is an excellent way to produce healthy food in a hurry.

If you have access to abundant fruit and vegetables, a child in the family who won't eat them, or an elderly person who can't chew them, a juicer is an excellent way of ensuring maximum intake of nutrients in a completely painless way.

Good quality stainless steel pans are a must, and one which has two steamer pans to go on top means that all the vegetables can be done on one ring. Two sizes of frying or sauté pan are useful, both with well-fitting lids.

A range of good-quality (and well-sharpened!) knives will do the job of many a gadget and of course, a range of wooden spatulas are indispensable.

Fabulous Fats

3

It is now well known that a high fat diet can cause many chronic health problems, but what is perhaps less well known is that low, or no fat diets also bring their own set of problems. We can certainly do without saturated fats, as the body is quite capable of converting them from polyunsaturated ones. What we cannot do without are the **essential fatty acids**, so called because, while they are essential to life, we cannot synthesize them ourselves. There are two types of essential fatty acids; one is alpha linolenic acid (Omega 3) and the other is linoleic acid (Omega 6). Both types are needed for energy production, helping the body to obtain more oxygen. Without them, the metabolic rate decreases, thereby encouraging weight gain rather than weight loss. They help to elevate mood and lift depression, and a deficiency in children can lead to hyperactivity and attention deficit disorder. They also play an important role in the health of the skin, hair and nails. They form a barrier in our skin against loss of moisture, so one of the first warning signs of low fatty acid status is a dry skin. In the cardiovascular system, Omega 3 fatty acids in the diet actually help to lower triglycerides by up to 65% and protect us from heart attacks and strokes. They are also required for healthy hormones; to carry the fat-soluble vitamins A, D and E; and so the list goes on - no wonder they can be called "Fabulous Fats"!

The main dietary sources of these fats are:

Omega 3 - found in oily fish such as salmon (preferably wild or sea salmon); trout; herrings; mackerel; sardines; pilchards; walnuts; linseeds, hemp and pumpkin seeds. If using walnut, linseed (flaxseed), hemp seed or pumpkin seed oil, do ensure that these are cold pressed as heat extraction of oils damages the chemical structure and turns them into **trans fats** (more about this shortly). Generally speaking, people nowadays are more likely to have a deficiency of these fats as they are so sadly lacking in the average diet.

Omega 6 - found in hemp seeds (roughly the same proportions as Omega 3), sunflower and sesame seeds, almonds, hazelnuts and Brazil nuts. Smaller amounts of Omega 6 fatty acids are also found in many other foods which are eaten to-day, and deficiency therefore tends to be less common.

I tend to make up a mixture of sunflower, sesame, pumpkin and two parts linseeds, which I keep in the fridge. Two tablespoons per day ground up in a coffee grinder and added to breakfast is the ideal way to ensure an adequate intake of essential fats, or you may use less and make up the difference with the appropriate nuts at another meal. Some people prefer to use an oil called "Essential Balance" which, as its name implies, contains a mixture of cold pressed oils in the correct ratio of about two parts Omega 3 to one part Omega 6. Two tablespoons per day are again recommended but should never be used in cooking.

The Benefits of Olive oil

Throughout this book, you will notice that we use olive oil for just about everything. Although it does not contain either Omega 3 or Omega 6 oils (it is in fact known as **Omega 9)**, a good Extra Virgin olive oil is cold pressed and unrefined, and it does not become damaged during the cooking process. It also forms a large part of the "Mediterranean Diet" which many believe to be one of the healthiest in the world.

The only other fat which is suitable for cooking, in small quantities, is butter which, although a saturated fat, does not have the disadvantage of turning into a trans-fat.

A word on trans-fats

There are three main processes which will turn our fabulous fats into killer fats, or trans fatty acids. The first and most common one is that of hydrogenation. This is mainly used to turn oils which have already been bleached, deodorized and refined into margarines which are cheap, spreadable and totally devoid of nutrients, but it is also used in vegetable shortenings. The second is frying in polyunsaturated oils. The delicate chemical structure is easily damaged at high temperature and can interfere with the way in which our cells function. The third process is the refining, deodorizing and bleaching of oils in order to increase their shelf-life. Unrefined sunflower oil, for example, is a rich golden brown which smells of sunflower seeds and has a short shelf-life (it should always be kept in the fridge); pumpkin seed oil is dark green and has the same short shelf-life.

When fresh oils are processed in this way, their molecules are damaged in such a way that the relevant receptor sites within the body are quite unable to recognize and utilize them. Not only that, but they actually prevent the uptake of the essential fatty acids.

If you wish to use some of the wonderful nut and seed oils, only do so in the form of a dressing. Buy them in small quantities, preferably in a dark bottle, store in the fridge, and use within a few weeks of opening.

As you will now realize, there really is no contest when it comes to the question of whether to use butter or margarine. Do, however, use the butter sparingly and preferably an organic one. If, however, you really do prefer margarine, always make sure that it is "non-hydrogenated" and don't use it for cooking.

.... And saturated fats.

These are usually easily recognized because they are mainly hard and of animal derivation. The main exception to this rule is coconut oil. In small quantities our body recognizes and utilizes them. They are natural and undamaged by processing, but as soon as we consume more than we can use, problems such as obesity and heart disease arise. They also interfere with the uptake of the all-important essential fatty acids, so do keep them to an absolute minimum - especially if your lifestyle is somewhat sedentary.

Dealing With Diets

4

It is not the brief of this book to give recipes which are specifically for people on various exclusion diets, but rather to enable you to adapt most recipes so that they can be enjoyed by anyone who has an allergy, intolerance or sensitivity to particular foods. We have, however, included just a few in order to show what can be done with alternative ingredients.

To-day, more and more people are finding that they have problems with certain foods, partly due to their previous over-consumption and partly due to the increasing pressures on their immune system, causing an inability to recognize such foods as part of a normal diet. An increasing problem is that of "leaky gut syndrome" in which molecules of food which should have been completely broken down and absorbed, and the remnants excreted, find their way through the gut wall and into the blood stream. As this is not the right place for such molecules, the body's defence system leaps into action causing a variety of symptoms from eczema to arthritis etc.

I find that the most common allergens are dairy products, wheat, gluten, sugar, coffee, oranges and yeast. Technically, true or "classical" allergy is one which causes the body to produce an antibody known as Immunoglobulin E (IgE). This often produces quite dramatic effects, leaving one in no doubt about the culprit. Increasingly, however, the antibody involved is Immunoglobulin G (IgG) and this does not usually cause an immediately noticeable effect. Instead, it may take anything up to 60 hours for a detrimental effect to occur, and in some cases it is the result of over-consumption of a particular food over many years. The on-set of such an intolerance may be triggered by a period of stress, either physical or emotional, when an already loaded immune system simply becomes over-loaded and no longer able to cope.

DAIRY PRODUCTS

Intolerance of dairy products, and in particular cows' milk and its derivatives, is becoming increasingly common in people of all ages, from babyhood to old age. It is a contributing factor in such varied disorders as irritable bowel syndrome, asthma, eczema, hyperactivity and inability to concentrate in young children, inability to lose weight, joint pains, rhinitis, insomnia, nausea and vomiting, catarrhal conditions, and so the list goes on.

In the Western world, dairy farming is a huge industry and, apart from being encouraged to drink our "daily pinta", it is added to many other foods to "enrich" them. If you see any of the following items listed as an ingredient in a food, it will not be milk-free:

Milk solids	lactose (milk sugar)	curds
Lactic acid	milk protein	whey
Casein	caseinate	

Foods which do, or may, contain dairy products, include:

Skimmed milk	dried milk	cheese
Scrambled eggs	BREAD (always check with the baker)	omelettes
Cream	yoghurt	butter
Evaporated/condensed milk	Coffeemate	soups
	baking powder	margarine
Cakes, buns, biscuits	chocolate	custard
Pudding mixes	sweets	chocolate
Pancakes	creamed foods	ice cream
Junket	cake toppings	dandelion coffee
Salad dressings	spreads	mashed potato

Because of the difference in size of the molecules contained in goats' and ewes' milk and cheese, some people find that they are able to tolerate them. On the whole, however, it is better to avoid all animal milks; after all, even young animals for whom the milk was intended by nature, discontinue its intake after a few months of age. Contrary to popular belief, it is not the best source of calcium. True it is very high in calcium, but then cows have a quite different bone structure to human beings. The protein content of cows' milk is higher than that of human breast milk; its phosphorus to calcium, and calcium to magnesium ratios are higher; (calcium cannot actually be metabolized without sufficient magnesium); its saturated fat content is higher; and its levels of essential fatty acids are lower. In other words, the balance of nutrients is not ideal for human beings. The cuisine of the world's largest population, the Chinese, does not include any dairy products, and yet they have hardly any osteoporosis, and lower incidences of other degenerative diseases.

It is very easy nowadays to buy alternative "milks" and every supermarket sells soya "milk". Health Food shops often have a variety of soya drinks, as well as oat milk, rice milk and dried pea milk. I am often asked if these alternatives taste like cows' milk, and of course they do not. However, once you become accustomed to the new taste, you may well find that you prefer it.

Any recipe which uses milk can simply be adapted to use one of the substitutes, either alone or diluted with water, although in fact we rarely include milk in any of our recipes.

The main concern of most people on a dairy-free diet is "how will I get sufficient calcium?" This should not be a problem if a wide variety of the following foods are included in the diet:

Sesame seeds	tinned salmon	chick peas	spring greens
Sunflower seeds	whitebait	black beans	kale
Tofu	sardines	pinto beans	root vegetables
Soya beans and TVP	pilchards	spinach	molasses
Brazil nuts	dried figs	buckwheat	watercress.

If you are still worried about your calcium intake, you may have calcium enriched soya milk or take a supplement. If doing the latter, however, it is important that you take this in an easily absorbed form such as calcium citrate, and always combined with magnesium in the correct ratio.

Milk intolerance problems relate to an inability to digest lactose (milk sugar) and/or the protein part (casein), but malabsorption of the fats may also cause a problem. I always recommend that people who have a dairy intolerance carry with them a specific milk-digesting enzyme for use on those occasions when they find it difficult to avoid dairy products.

Dairy (and wheat) free white sauce

2 tbsp extra virgin olive oil
1 small onion, finely chopped
2 oz (50g) sunflower seeds.

½ pint (250 mls) vegetable stock
Seasoning if required

Heat oil in a small pan - don't *over*heat. Add onion and cook gently until soft and golden. Add sunflower seeds and cook until lightly coloured. Add stock and simmer 5 minutes.

Liquidize until smooth and serve with any dish normally requiring a white sauce, or with baked potato and stir-fry vegetables.

Banana and coconut milk ice cream

2 large, ripe bananas
2 oz/50g raspberries or strawberries

¾ pint/400 ml tinned coconut milk

Purée bananas in a food processor with the coconut milk. Mix in the berries and a little date syrup if not sweet enough. Turn into an ice-cream maker and churn freeze. Serve slightly soft.

Bitter chocolate and coconut ice cream

10oz/300g dairy free chocolate
¾ pint/400ml coconut milk

Melt the chocolate in a double boiler (or in a glass bowl standing in a pan of hot water). Gradually add the coconut milk and heat together until totally blended. Cool to room temperature. Pour into an ice cream maker if you have one and churn freeze. If you do not have an ice-cream maker, partially freeze, remove from the freezer and beat well in a food processor. Return to the freezer. Serve before it is totally frozen, or freeze for future use. To use, allow to soften in the fridge for at least 30 minutes.

Kiwi, lime and banana frozen yoghurt

8 oz/225g Provamel Yofu (soya yoghurt) or Greek-style yoghurt if permitted
2 kiwi fruit, peeled
1 ripe banana
juice of 1-2 limes

Purée the kiwi fruit, banana and lime juice in a food processor. Add the yoghurt. If you have an ice cream maker, pour the mixture in and churn/freeze till ready. Serve at once or, if stored in the freezer, allow to soften in the fridge for 20 minutes before serving.

WHEAT

Wheat is one of the most common allergens, intolerances or sensitivities in the Western diet to-day. It is eaten by most people every day and, in some cases, at every meal.

A wheat-free diet should not be confused with a gluten-free diet, as certain gluten-free products may contain other fractions of wheat than gluten. Conversely, if your allergy is to wheat rather than gluten, you may well be able to eat such foods as oats, barley and rye, although preferably in minimal quantities. Anyone who has a food intolerance of one kind often has a tendency to become intolerant of other, frequently eaten foods, so as wide a variety as possible should be included in the diet.

Wheat is a relatively new food - we have only had 10,000 years to get used to it, which is the blinking of an eye in evolutionary terms. Although natural selection should gradually eliminate any genes that make human beings susceptible to wheat, it seems to be a process that has not had time to be completed. This has not been helped by the fact that, since 1900, wheat and other cereals have been hybridized to produce strains which have the better grading and baking qualities required by the food industry but are more difficult for the digestive system to cope with.

Wheat is cheap and easy to grow and is therefore included as an unnecessary "filler" by some food manufacturers. For example, if you were to make your own chutney, you would not add wheat, but many commercial manufacturers do just that. For this reason, it is important to read very carefully the ingredients of all manufactured foods, and particularly the following:

Baked beans (except Whole Earth and Heinz)	Baking powder	batter mixes
Blancmange powders	biscuits	breadcrumbed foods
Cakes	chocolate (cheap brands)	chutney
Cocoa	cornflour (corn starch)	crispbreads
Curry powder	custard	gravy powder & mixes
Ice cream (cheap brands)	macaroni	muesli (some)
Mustard	Pancakes	pasta
Pastry	Porridge (some)	sandwich spreads
Sauces	Soy sauce (except La Choy)	stock cubes

For some people, a small amount of wheat contained in these foods may be tolerated, but for others, a considerable reaction will be experienced.

Avoid all ingredients listed as:

Edible starch	food starch	thickening
Rusk	Bran	hydrolyzed starch
Monosodium Glutamate (msg)	crumb	

Fortunately, there are many alternatives, and the first thing to do when you start a wheat-free diet is to make sure that your store cupboard contains a good variety of these:

Truefree flours are guaranteed wheat-free and come in different packs for specific purposes, including bread-making.

Terence Stamp's Wheat-free flour

Ryvita and rye bread. Do make sure that these are 100% rye, some are not.

Oat cakes. Again, check the ingredients. Many brands are made with part wheat.

Cereals: muesli, but again, check the ingredients - it is preferable to make your own following the recipes in The Big Breakfast section.

Flour: for general cooking purposes such as thickening sauces, pastry making etc., the following types of flour are available and may be used alone or in combination:

Arrowroot	Barley	Buckwheat (a pulse, not wheat)
Chestnut	Chick pea (gram flour)	Maize (corn)
Millet	Potato	Rye
Sago	Soya	Quinoa

With a little planning, a wheat-free diet is not nearly as daunting as it first appears! And particularly if you spend a little time batch-baking for the freezer:

Wheat-free soda bread

8 oz/225g permitted flour	4 oz olive oil (weigh a measuring jug and pour in the oil)
1 egg	1 tea cup soya, rice or oat milk
4 tsp. baking powder	You may also like to add a grated carrot and/or a handful of seeds

Dissolve the baking powder in the milk. Mix all other ingredients together well. Add milk/baking powder SLOWLY - DO NOT KNEAD. Put mixture into a greased loaf tin and bake in oven Gas Mark 5 or electric 370°F/190°C for 45-60 minutes or until firm to touch (test with a skewer).

Scones

Use the above recipe but without the egg. Add the milk very slowly as you may find you need less.

Biscuits

Make as for scones, but add your choice of seeds, nuts, dried fruit or dates.

Bran

If you really do feel the need to add this to your diet, use soya or rice bran, and always with plenty of fluids. Linseeds or Psyllium seed husks have a more gently laxative effect.

Pasta

There is now a wonderful array of non-wheat pasta available at most Health Food Shops. These include: rice, spelt, millet, barley, buckwheat and corn, but a **word of warning:** you really must follow the cooking directions for each individual variety. Sometimes they need very little cooking and that extra minute can change a delicious food into a soggy mass.

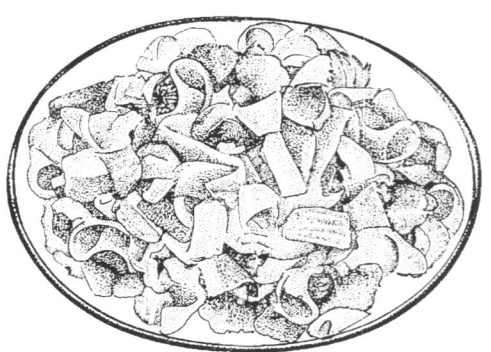

Pasta with celery and almond sauce

Use 2 oz/50g millet, buckwheat, rice, barley or spelt pasta per person. Cook strictly according to instructions on the packet.

Sauce:

- 4 tbsp olive oil
- 8 oz/225g onions, chopped
- 8 oz/225g celery, finely chopped
- 2 cloves garlic
- ¼ pint/150ml vegetable stock
- Seasoning if required
- 4 oz/125g slivered almonds

Heat olive oil and fry onions, celery and garlic gently until really tender. Add stock, cover and cook for a further 5-10 minutes until sauce is creamy. Season to taste.

Place almonds in grill pan and toast until lightly browned (be careful - they burn easily). Serve the sauce over freshly cooked pasta; sprinkle with almonds.

Rye muffins

- 8oz/225g rye flour
- 2 tbsp raw cane sugar
- 4 fl oz water
- 2 tsp baking powder
- ¼ tsp salt
- 2 tbsp olive oil

Preheat the oven to 400°F/200°C/Gas Mark 6. Sift the flour and baking powder and stir in the sugar. Add cold water and mix until smooth. Stir in the oil and pour into six paper muffin cups. Bake for 20-25 minutes.

Rice biscuits

6 oz/175g rice flour (or oat meal or maize meal)
1 oz/25g currants
3 oz/75g raw cane sugar, molasses or honey
2 tbsp olive oil
2 free range eggs

Beat eggs, sugar/honey/molasses. Add rice flour and currants, previously mixed. Beat well, roll out and cut into shapes/fingers. Bake on a floured tin at 300°/180°(Gas Mark 3).

Oatcakes

Although this is essentially a book for busy people (who may prefer to go out and buy their oatcakes), there is no doubt that home-made ones taste so much better. Perhaps you could get the kids to make these!

8 oz/225g mixed oatmeals- fine, medium and pinhead
3 ½ oz/100g gram (chick pea) flour
1 level teaspoon wheat-free baking powder
3 oz/75g olive oil or butter

Put the oatmeal into a food processor and sift in the gram flour and baking powder. Add oil and process to a stiff dough with a little cold water. Turn out onto a board sprinkled with oatmeal and roll out thinly. Cut into rounds or squares and place on a tray. Bake in a moderate oven (170°C/350°F/Gas Mark 4) for 20-25 minutes. Cool on a rack and store in an airtight container or in the freezer.

Bran and apple tea bread

3 oz/75g oat bran   4 oz/125g raw cane sugar

4 oz/125g raisins   4 oz/125g chopped apple

½ pint/300ml soya milk or apple juice (if using apple juice, reduce sugar to 2 oz)

8 oz/225g Spelt or a combination of other, permitted flours.

Soak bran, sugar, fruits, soya milk/juice overnight. Next day, add flour. Stir well and bake in greased tin for 1-1 ¼ hours at 225° F (Gas Mark 2)

When cool, slice and spread with a little butter or non-hydrogenated margarine. Keep a few slices in the freezer, individually wrapped ready for a lunch box or snack.

Chocolate cake

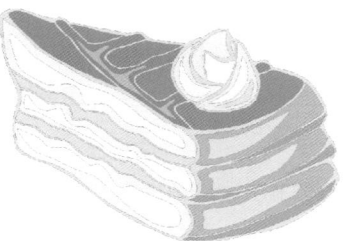

5 ½ oz/150g olive oil

5 ½ g/150g softened dried dates

2 tbsp boiling water

2 heaped tbsp Black and Green's chocolate powder

3 eggs

3 oz/75g gram (chick pea) flour sifted with 2 tsp wheat and gluten free baking powder

2 tbsp soya or coconut milk

Liquidize the olive oil and dates. When well amalgamated, transfer to a bowl. Melt the chocolate powder in the boiling water, then stir into the mixture. Stir in the eggs alternately with a spoonful of flour. Fold in the rest of the flours and the baking powder. Transfer to a well oiled cake tin lined with greaseproof paper and bake in a moderate oven (350ºF/180ºC/Gas Mark 4) for 35 minutes or until a skewer comes out clean. Turn out onto a rack to cool.

Apple and cashew nut cake

5 ½ oz/150g olive oil
7 oz/200g grated fresh dessert apples
3 ½ oz/100g gram (chick pea) flour sifted with
3 tsp wheat and gluten-free baking powder

2 oz/50g softened dried dates
3 ½ oz/100g ground cashew nuts,
juice of 1 small orange

In a food processor, whiz the oil with the dates and apples. When they are really well amalgamated, transfer to a bowl. Fold in the cashew nuts, the flour sifted with the baking powder and the orange juice.

Transfer to a well oiled cake tin lined with greaseproof paper and bake in a moderate oven (350ºF/180ºC/Gas Mark 4) for 45-50 minutes or until a skewer comes out clean. Turn out onto a rack to cool.

Pastry - oat-based

8 oz/225g jumbo or porridge oats, powdered in a grinder or food processor
125g/5oz butter or olive oil

Rub butter if using, in to powdered oats, or mix in olive oil. Using your hands, line an 8" flan dish and either bake blind for 20 minutes at 325°F/160°C or Gas Mark 3 until pastry is tanned, or use as required.

Pastry rice based

8oz/225g fine rice flour
6oz/175g grated apple

4oz/125g butter or olive oil

Blend, knead and flatten onto a dish or plate. Fill with fruit or chosen filling.

GLUTEN

As well as being found in wheat, it is also contained in oats, barley and rye. Gluten-free flours and other dietary products are usually made from grains which are processed in order to take out the gluten. These may include wheat so that a gluten-free product is not necessarily wheat-free. Fortunately, many such products are both wheat- and gluten-free.

Flours which are naturally gluten-free include:

> Rice; chick pea; soya; millet, maize flour (cornmeal), potato, chestnut, qunioia and pea.
> *Trufree* flours are both wheat- and gluten-free.

Rice porridge

½ pint/¼ litre milk, soya, rice or oat milk
1 tbs raisins, chopped dates or apricots

2 tbsp brown ground rice or rice flakes
½ oz/15 grams ground almonds

Put the milk and rice into a saucepan and stir until smooth. Add the dried fruit and heat to boiling point. Stir constantly until the rice is cooked and the fruit plump. Add the almonds, stir well and serve hot with a little extra milk.

This can also be made with millet flakes.

Gram (chickpea) pancakes

4 oz/125 g gram flour
12 fl oz/350ml cold water

1 pinch of salt
Olive oil for frying

Mix the flour and salt together. Gradually add the water until a smooth batter is formed. Heat a little oil in a frying pan, add a quarter of the batter, and cook until the edges are crispy and brown and the top is cooked. Serve with either a savoury, or fruity, filling.

Buttermilk scones

225g/8oz buckwheat flour
¼ tsp baking powder
½ pint/300ml buttermilk

2 oz /50g olive oil
a pinch of sea salt

Sieve the flour, salt and baking powder into a bowl. Mix well and stir in the olive oil. Add sufficient buttermilk to make a loose dough. Knead lightly, shape and place on a greased baking tin at 425°F/220°C/ Gas Mark 7 for 25-20 minutes. Transfer to a cooling rack.

Potato cakes

½ lb/225g cooked potatoes
1 tbsp olive oil
¼ tsp baking powder

2 oz /50g buckwheat (or millet or rice) flour
a pinch of sea salt
milk or soya milk

Put the flour, salt and baking powder into a food processor. Mix well and add the potatoes and olive oil. Process to a smooth dough, adding a little milk if required. Shape into cakes and cook on a hot, oiled, griddle until brown on both sides.

Spiced currant cookies

4 oz/125 grams brown ground rice flour

3 oz/75 grams grated apple

½ tsp mixed spice

2 fl oz/50 mls olive oil

1½ oz/40g raw cane sugar

1½ oz/40g currants

Preheat oven to 450°F/230°C (Gas Mark 8)

Blend the ground rice and olive oil with a fork. Add the apple, sugar, spice and currants. Knead into a large ball.
Grease a baking sheet. Divide the dough into ten and shape with a knife or spatula. Bake for 20-25 minutes, then allow to cool a little on the baking sheet before moving onto a cooling tray.

SUGAR

Comparatively few people are actually allergic to sugar, but most of us would benefit from reducing it to the absolute minimum.

In the past two hundred years, sugar production has increased 400 times, from ¼ million tonnes in 1800 to over 100 million tonnes per year in the 1990's. The average British adult consumes about 70 lbs (32 kilos) of sugar every year and although many people have stopped adding sugar to food and drinks, the overall consumption of sugar remains the same. This indicates a high level of "hidden" sugars in foods such as baked beans, savoury biscuits and many other processed foods. More sweets and chocolates are consumed per head in Britain than in any other country.

Sugar contains no nutrients, no fibre, and nothing which the human body actually requires. It has been identified as one of the main causes of excess weight and dental cavities and increases the risk of heart disease, high blood pressure, low blood sugar (hypoglycaemia) and diabetes. It is also implicated in hyperactivity and lack of concentration, aggressive behaviour and many other disorders. The word "sugar" does not always appear on labels. Instead, the sugar content may be broken down, so that it appears less, into some of the following ingredients:

Sucrose	glucose	glucose syrup
Dextrose	maltose	

Believe it or not, your taste buds will gradually adjust to a sugar-free diet and within months, or even weeks, foods which you used to enjoy will taste far too sweet.

In the meantime, there are plenty of alternatives:

Fresh fruit	dried fruits such as raisins, apricots, figs, prunes
Tinned fruit in natural juice	apple juice for sweetening
Date syrup for cooking	sugar-free jams
Sugar-free baked beans	

Honey, if pure, is not as concentrated as sugar, but do not rush in and add it in large quantities. It will perpetuate a sweet tooth and contains very few nutrients. Most commercial varieties come from bees which have been fed on white sugar.

Fruit Bars need to be chosen with care as some of them are excessively sweet. Try to buy those with a good portion of nuts as well.

Artificial Sweeteners. Quite apart from the fact that these prolong the dependency on sweet food, research studies have linked artificial sweeteners in general and Aspartame in particular, with serious health problems. Aspartame undergoes a complex conversion path after its ingestion, leading to the production of substances such as formaldehyde and formic acid within the body. Our bodies were not designed to metabolize chemicals such as aspartame, saccharine and sorbitol, and there is some suggestion that their inclusion in your diet will actually increase the desire for sugar - as if the body has somehow been cheated and wants recompense.

Fructose or fruit sugar is a better alternative as you beginning the weaning off process, but only in moderation. Fructose has to be broken down into glucose before the body can use it as fuel, and consequently it is metabolized slightly more slowly.

Fructo-oligosaccharides (FOS)

Although this comes in the form of a sweet, white, powder, it is actually a natural fibre that occurs in raw fruits and vegetables. It has the added advantages of supporting the growth of beneficial intestinal bacteria; providing very few calories; and not elevating blood sugar levels. In fact, its only real drawback is that it may cause a certain amount of wind in some people.

Fruit and nut energy bars

4 oz/125g mixed nuts
A little apple or orange juice.

Finely grind nuts and put into food processor with chopped fruits. Bind with fruit juice.

Sugar-free flapjacks

100 grams/4 oz apple concentrate

225 grams/9 oz jumbo or porridge oats

50grams/2 oz pine kernels or sunflower seeds

100 grams/4oz olive oil

Mix the olive oil with the fruit concentrate. Lightly process the oats in a food processor or liquidizer. Stir the oats, nuts and/or seeds into the oil and concentrate and mix well together. Press the mixture into greased tin and cook for 20 minutes in a cool oven (350ºF/150ºC/Gas Mark 3) or until they are lightly browned. As soon as they are cooked, section them with a knife and allow to cool. Remove carefully from the tin as they are very crumbly, and store in a box or in the freezer.

If you feel that you need more help and ideas with particular diets, I would suggest that you contact Berrydales Publishers, 5 Lawns Road, London NW3 2XS. Tel. 020 7722 2866 E-mail: Berrydales@Compuserve.com. They provide an excellent publication called "*The Inside Story*", a special diet cookbook, and a list of Special Diet Food Suppliers. A yearly subscription costs £29.96

There is now a considerable number of books catering specifically for specialised diets. If your local bookshop is unable to help, ring the Nutri Centre Bookshop on 0207 323 2382.

Going Nuts? Running to Seed?

5

There is no doubt that nuts and seeds are super foods par excellence. Think of the vitality in, say, a sunflower seed that allows it to grow to its ultimate height, or a pumpkin seed which produces a plant capable of bearing several pumpkins. Most of them contain a good balance of protein, carbohydrate and essential fats.

SEEDS

A combination of different seeds can easily provide all the essential fatty acids which are required by the body for healthy functioning. Sunflower and sesame seeds are high in Omega 6 fatty acids; while pumpkin and flax, or linseeds, contain abundant Omega 3 fatty acids - the same family of fats as fish oils - thereby making them an extremely useful addition to the diet of someone who does not eat fish. They are high in minerals - particularly zinc, magnesium and calcium - and sesame and sunflower seeds are also rich in selenium and vitamin E, thereby making a useful contribution to the anti-oxidant, cancer-fighting, army of the body.

Hemp Seeds (not for growing!!)

Hemp seed has been described by many as a "super-food" and has been an important food source for many cultures over time. Hemp seeds are actually more accurately described as "nuts", delicious roasted on their own, but mainly used to make milk, tofu, flour, butter and pasta. Hemp is comparable to soya beans for protein content, but, as yet, there has been no genetic engineering of hemp. They are also said to be as versatile as the soya bean; even more nutritious; and easier to digest. In addition they provide an ideal balance of essential fatty acids, protein and carbohydrates, so are perfect for between-meal snacks.

Hemp oil contains many of the Essential Fatty Acids that the body requires for optimum health, and they come in exactly the right ratio for maximum absorption.

If you have difficulty finding hemp seeds and hemp seed products in your local health food shop, they are obtainable from The Hemp Shop, 22 Gardner St, Brighton BN1 1UP telephone 07041 313233, or visit their web site at **www.thehempshop.com** They also produce a book "*Hemp Foods and Oil for Health*" which gives some excellent recipes.

NUTS

So many people deprive themselves of the health benefits of eating nuts because they have the reputation of being fattening. True, the calorific value of nuts is relatively high, but adding 1-2 tbsp. to breakfast can improve blood sugar levels to such an extent that you don't need that bar of chocolate, with far more calories, later in the day. The oils they contain are the essential ones, so that the body is able to utilize the nutrients rather than just storing them as fat, unlike the saturated fat which is found in chocolate, biscuits and cakes. Almonds are a particularly good source of Omega 6, and walnuts provide ample Omega 3 fatty acids, both of which should be in balance in the diet. On the whole, most people tend to be deficient in the latter, partly due to the fact that we now eat far less cold-water, oily fish than in the past. Hazelnuts have the lowest fat content of all nuts. Brazil nuts are high in the mineral selenium.

Nut butters such as almond, cashew and hazelnut are excellent for a snack, with oat or rice cakes, Ryvita or a chunk of wholemeal or rye bread.

Peanuts

Strictly speaking, these are not nuts, but are a type of groundnut. They are, however, high in protein and a useful snack or addition to salads. Try buying them unsalted and roast them lightly on an oven tray.

Because I get through such quantities of seeds, I tend to buy them in bulk (1-2 kg at a time). Left on a shelf or in the cupboard, they would go rancid, causing free-oxidising radicals to damage their delicate structure, quite apart from tasting less good. Immediately after buying them, I spend a little time putting them into, say, 8 oz/225g packets, and putting one bag of each into the fridge and the others into the freezer. Nuts and seeds freeze wonderfully well. I then put a mixture of equal amounts of sunflower, pumpkin, sesame and linseeds into a jar and have them in some form at breakfast time - preferably ground finely in order to release all their goodness rather than have some of them pass whole through the colon. They can also be sprinkled on salads or added to soup. Although generally speaking it is best to eat them raw, they can be put into "healthy" cakes and biscuits containing large amounts of other good ingredients and small amounts of sugar and give an interesting texture to crumbles. Nut burgers and nut roasts are an excellent source of protein for vegans and vegetarians.

Sprouting

Seeds can also be sprouted, and even if you don't have time to do this, it could be fun for children to do so. When sprouted, a chemical reaction takes place which multiplies the vitamin and protein content and also makes them more digestible. Soya beans, which are poisonous when raw, are perfectly safe when sprouted. The simplest and least labour-intensive way of doing this is to go and buy a sprouter from a good health food shop. Soak sunflower, pumpkin, unhulled sesame, or alfalfa seeds overnight or for several hours in filtered or spring water; drain really well and arrange on the trays of the sprouter. Keep in a warm place and do remember to water them - preferably with a spray. Rinse the seeds once a day. They will be ready in a few days, but generally the sprout should be about 1-2"/3-5mm long. (the smaller the seed, the quicker it will sprout). If after three to five days you find there are too many to use immediately, put them into a bag or box in the fridge.

If you are new to sprouting, a good one to start with is alfalfa. The weight of the sprouts is many times that of the seeds, and they are a really nutritious addition to a salad or a sandwich.

RECIPES

Watercress and walnut salad

1 bunch of watercress, carefully washed and dried
1 head of chicory
3 tbsp walnut oil
freshly ground black pepper and sea salt

3 oz/75mg chopped walnuts
2 tbsp Balsamic vinegar
1 orange

Chop up the watercress and chicory. Add walnuts, and the orange, peeled and cut into small segments. Mix the oil, vinegar, salt and pepper in a screw top jar. Shake vigorously and dress the salad.

Nutty lentil paté

8 oz/225 grams red lentils
2 tbsp olive oil
1-2 tsp mixed herbs
Seasoning to taste

1 medium onion
¾ pint/420 mls vegetable stock
3 oz/75grams walnut pieces

Heat the oil and gently sauté the finely chopped onion. Add the lentils and cook a minute longer. Pour in the stock, seasoning and herbs, bring to the boil and simmer until all the water has been absorbed. Set aside to cool. Meanwhile, grind the nuts. Mash the lentils, or put into a food processor, add the nuts and turn into a serving dish. Chill.

Nut butter

Almonds or cashew nuts
Cold-pressed sunflower, safflower, walnut or hazelnut oil
A little grated lemon rind for flavour

Grind the fresh or lightly roasted nuts (finely or coarsely according to taste). Gradually add drops of the preferred oil until a spreading consistency is obtained. Add the lemon rind and mix thoroughly.

This makes an excellent snack on wholemeal toast, rice or oatcakes, or Ryvita.

Peanut butter

Raw or lightly toasted peanuts
Olive oil
Sea Salt

Grind the peanuts - until either floury or crunchy, according to the texture required. Add enough oil to make a thick paste and add a little sea salt to taste. Another excellent snack as above, or with apple slices.

Sunflower seed spread

4 oz/100 g ground sunflower seeds
2 oz/50g peanut butter
1-2 tbsp olive oil
Soy sauce or tamari to taste

Mix together the ground seeds and peanut butter. Add sufficient oil to get the required consistency, and soya sauce or tamari to taste.

Tahini spread

Tahini is another type of "butter", but made purely from sesame seeds - an excellent source of calcium. It comes in both light and dark types, the dark variety being made from unhulled seeds and tasting slightly chocolatey. It can be spread just as it is, or, for a stronger flavoured spread try the following recipe:

8 tbsp tahini
2 tbsp miso
Sufficient water to make a creamy paste
Grated rind of half a lemon.

Mix the tahini and miso together and very gradually add water - rather like making mayonnaise - until creamy.

Nut "milk"

4 oz/125g blanched almonds
1 pint/600mls water
Honey to taste

Blend all ingredients until creamy

Nut cream

6 oz/175g cashew nuts
¼ pint/150mls cold water
Natural honey to taste

Grind the nuts very finely; add the water and honey (if required).

Cashew, hazelnut or almond and sunflower spread

3 oz/75g nuts   2 oz/50g sunflower seeds
Cold-pressed walnut oil.

Grind the nuts and seeds very finely. Mix well and add sufficient oil to give a spreading texture.

Hemp milk

8oz/225g hulled hempseeds   40 fl oz water
Optional flavourings: vanilla, maple syrup, carob or honey.

Blend water and hulled seeds in an electric blender until completely smooth and creamy. Add any required flavouring and a pinch of sea salt to bring out the flavour.

Liz's nut roast (as requested frequently by my children)

12 oz/350g cooked brown rice   6 oz/175g coarsely ground nuts and seeds
2 eggs   1 onion, finely chopped
1 large carrot, and/or courgette, grated   1 tbsp. tamari
herbs, as available

Fry the onion, carrot and/or courgette in olive oil until soft. Remove from heat and combine with other ingredients. Put into an oiled loaf tin and cook at 350ºF/180ºC/Gas Mark 4 for 45-60 minutes, until firm to touch. Turn out onto a tray.

The wonderful thing about this recipe is that it takes very little longer to make two loaves. What you don't eat hot can be sliced; each slice individually wrapped; and frozen. Excellent for lunches with salad, picnics etc.

Hemp and almond pesto

4 fl oz/125g toasted, hulled hempseeds
1 bunch basil
3 tbsp olive oil

6oz/175g cup sliced almonds
1 tbsp hemp oil
2 cups grated parmesan cheese

Crush the seeds, almonds, basil, hemp oil and olive oil to a paste with a pestle in a mortar. Mix in the parmesan. Heat the pesto gently, being careful not to cook it, and serve with your favourite pasta.

Juicy carrot salad

8 large carrots
6 tbsp hemp oil
2-3" (3-5mm) fresh ginger

4 tbsp hulled hempseeds
2 tbsp lemon juice
sea salt

Grate the carrots. Toast the seeds lightly and add them to the carrot. Press the ginger in a garlic press and combine it with all the other ingredients. Pour the sauce over the carrots and seeds and toss well. Let the salad sit for at least half an hour before serving.

Hempseed Tahini

8oz/225g hulled hempseeds
1 tbsp water (optional)

1 tbsp hemp oil

Toast the seeds and finely grind them in a blender. Combine them with the oil and mix to a smooth paste. The mixture may require some water to keep it moist. Delicious as a snack on wholemeal toast, oatcakes or rice cakes, or may be used to make Hempseed Hummus.

Hempseed hummus

6oz/175g hempseed tahini
1 tbsp hemp oil
3-4 cloves garlic
freshly ground pepper

15oz/425g tin of cooked chickpeas
4fl oz juice of a lemon
1 tsp soy sauce
a pinch of cayenne pepper (optional)

Purée the chickpeas in a blender; add the other ingredients; blend until the texture is smooth and creamy.

Chick pea and walnut salad

1 400g (14oz) tin chick peas
2 tbsp fresh lemon juice
2 cloves garlic (optional)

125g (4 oz) walnuts
4 tbsp Extra Virgin olive oil
Sea salt to taste

Drain, rinse and mash the chick peas. Chop the walnuts (or grind coarsely in a coffee grinder). Combine the oil, lemon juice, garlic if used, and salt, and mix this dressing with the walnuts and chick peas. Serve with a large, green salad / crusty bread or oat cakes.

Cashew nut roast

8 oz/225g ground cashew nuts (or a mixture of any nuts)
4 oz/100g mushrooms
2 tbsp rice flour
½ pint milk or soya milk

1 egg
1 onion, finely chopped
1 tbsp olive oil
¼ tsp mixed herbs

Gently warm the olive oil and cook the onion and mushrooms for 3-4 minutes. Gradually add the rice flour, stirring all the time. Do the same with the milk. Cool slightly and add a beaten egg and the nuts and herbs. Put into a baking dish and cook in a medium oven for about 40 minutes, or until firm to touch.

Almond stuffed mushrooms

Allow 2-3 mushrooms per person, depending on size.

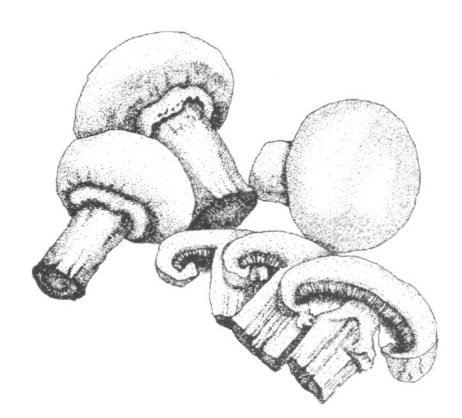

For the stuffing (per person):

Half a slice of wholemeal bread (or 2 tbsp oatmeal and a little boiling water)
6 almonds , chopped or coarsely ground in a coffee grinder
Rind of half a lemon
Fresh chopped parsley
1 tbsp sunflower or pumpkin seeds (or a combination of the two)
1 tbsp olive oil.

Remove and chop the stems from the mushrooms. Lightly oil a baking tray and place the mushrooms, wiped, on it. Crumb the bread in a blender or coffee grinder. Add all the other ingredients and mix together briefly. Stuff into the mushroom and drizzle a little olive oil over each. Place in a hot oven and cook for about 15 minutes. The mushrooms should be soft and the stuffing crisp.

Thickening soup

When making soup, fry a chopped onion in a little olive oil until soft, add 1 tbsp sunflower seeds and cook until light brown, add other vegetables, then stock. Simmer 10-15 minutes. Liquidize and you will have a thick and creamy soup with a good helping of protein.

Celery and almond sauce

4tbs olive oil
8oz/225g onions, diced
8 oz/225g celery, finely chopped

1/4 pint/150ml light vegetable stock
seasoning to taste
2 cloves garlic

Heat the olive oil and fry the onions and celery with the garlic over gentle heat 2-3 mins. Cover and continue cooking 10-15 mins until vegetables are tender. Add stock, cover and cook for another 5-10 minutes until creamy. Serve with freshly cooked pasta, topped with 1 oz slivered almonds (lightly roasted in the oven) per person.

Chicken and walnut casserole

4 chicken pieces
1 onion
3 ½ oz/100 grams walnut pieces
1 glass sherry or vermouth
1 tbs. fresh tarragon, or 2 tsp dried tarragon)
½ pint (300 mls) water
2 tbsp olive oil

Heat the olive oil in a deep sauté pan or ovenware casserole dish. Add the chicken pieces and brown them on all sides. Remove and add chopped onion. Cook lightly until transparent. Add 1 tbsp flour, cook for a couple of minutes and then add water, stirring to make a sauce. Add the walnut pieces. Cover and allow to simmer for approx. 45-50 minutes. Alternatively, cook in a moderate oven (350ºF/180º/Gas Mark 4) for at least 1 hour.

Spiced lamb and aubergines

For four people.

1½ lb (700 grams) diced lamb
1 onion
1 tbsp garam marsala
1 carton of Greek yoghurt

1 large aubergine
3 oz/75g ground almonds
1 pint (600mls) water

Cut the aubergine into chunks the same size as the lamb pieces. Put lamb, chopped up onion and aubergine in an ovenware dish. Add the almonds. Place in a moderate oven and cook for about 45 minutes. Stir in the garam marsala and the yoghurt and return to the oven. Cook for a further 10 minutes, until most of the liquid is absorbed. Alternatively, cook on top of the stove, simmering gently, and then turning up the heat to reduce the liquid.

Sprouted seed salad

200g/8 oz sprouted seeds
 (sunflower, alfalfa, fenugreek, green lentil etc.)
2 tsp grated ginger
2 tsp tamari

1 yellow pepper, chopped
1 red pepper, chopped
½ tsp fennel seeds
2 tbsp Essential Balance or Udo's oil

Combine the sprouts and peppers. Whisk the remaining ingredients together and pour over. Gently toss to mix.

Nut pilaf

- 225g/8 oz Basmati rice
- 1 tbsp olive oil
- 1 tbsp butter
- 1-2 cloves garlic, crushed
- 5 tbsp mixed nuts, chopped
- 1.2 litres/2 pints vegetable stock
- 1 onion, chopped
- seasoning to taste
- juice and zest of 1 orange
- 2 tbsp parsley, chopped

Cook the rice in the stock until just tender, and then drain. Heat the butter and oil and gently cook the onion and garlic. Add the orange juice and rice, and mix well. Stir in the nuts and parsley and mix well together before serving.

Fennel and almond soup

- 4 fennel bulbs
- 1 leek
- 50g/2 oz butter
- 1.2 litres/2 pints vegetable stock
- 4 tbsp freshly ground almond
- sea salt and black pepper

Remove the tough outer layers from the fennel and chop the remaining bulb into small pieces. Remove the outer leaves from the leek and slice into rounds. Melt the butter and stir in the fennel and leek. Sweat gently for 5 minutes. Add the stock and bring to the boil. Simmer covered for 15-20 minutes. Add the ground almonds and cool slightly, then blend in a liquidizer until smooth. Adjust seasoning.

Almond apple pudding

1 lb/450g cooking apples
grated rind of a lemon
1 tbsp honey
3 oz /75g unrefined "castor" sugar

4 oz/100 g ground almonds
2 free range eggs
3 oz/75g butter
a pinch of cinnamon

Cream the butter and sugar. Add a spoonful of the almonds before adding the beaten eggs, mixing thoroughly, then add the rest of the almonds. Peel, core and slice the apples and place in a buttered casserole dish, along with the honey, lemon rind and cinnamon. Spoon the almond mixture on top and cook in a moderate oven 350°F/180°C/Gas Mark 4 for approx. 30 minutes. The top should be crisp and brown.

Nut brownies

1 free range egg white
2 ½ oz/65 g raw cane sugar
2 ½ oz/65g ground nuts: almonds, pecans, hazelnuts or walnuts
1 tbsp brown ground rice
Grated rind of half an orange
Rice paper

Preheat oven to 350°F/180°C, Gas Mark 4

Whisk the egg white until **stiff**; add the sugar and nuts. Stir in the ground rice and orange rind. Shape into rounds and place on rice paper on a baking sheet. Bake for 20-25 minutes.

Fruit and nut crumble

4 portions of stewed fruit, sweetened to taste with fructose (blackberry and apple works well)

2 tbs olive oil

1 oz /30g ground almonds

1 oz sunflower seeds

6 oz /150g ground brown rice

1 tbs raw cane sugar

Preheat oven to 425ºF/220ºC /Gas Mark 7

Put the stewed fruit into an ovenproof dish. Put all the other ingredients into a food processor and mix until they resemble fine breadcrumbs. Spoon the crumble over the stewed fruit and bake for 10-15 minutes until golden brown. Serve hot or cold with single cream, yoghurt or soya cream.

Walnut pavlova tart

2 oz /50g butter	3 ½ oz /100g unrefined brown sugar
1 egg yolk	3 ½ oz /100g wholemeal (or permitted) flour
2 egg whites	3 oz/75g chopped walnuts

Melt the butter and allow to cool. Stir in 1 oz sugar, egg yolk and flour. Knead lightly and press over base and side of a greased, 8 ½ inch/21cm greased pie plate. Whisk egg whites until stiff but not dry. Whisk in remainder of sugar. Fold in finely chopped walnuts. Spoon on to the pastry case. Bake at 350ºF/180ºC/Gas mark 4 for 30 minutes.

The filling will be well risen, but the meringue cracks slightly as it shrinks.

Treat Yourself To Tofu

6

The problem with tofu is its image! And the fact that we in the West have not been used to having it in our diet. Its advantages, however, are legion and I very often recommend its inclusion - even in the diets of meat-eaters. In fact, it really is truly a wonderfood, being both nutritious and versatile.

First of all - what exactly is it?

Tofu, or soyabean curd is made by soaking the beans in water, grinding them to a pulp, cooking and straining them to produce soya milk to which a coagulant is added. It comes in a fairly solid form, or a softer form known as "silken". Apart from the smoked or marinated forms, it has virtually no taste which, although a bit off-putting at first, is in fact a great advantage as it can be added to both sweet and savoury foods. It should be as fresh as possible, and any that remains from the block after first use should be kept in a bowl of water in the fridge, with the water being changed every day.

Why should I bother with it?

Tofu is the dieter's dream, being high in protein, low in saturated fats, sodium and calories and totally free of cholesterol. More than that, however, it is very high in compounds known as phytoestrogens. These have gentle, safe, and highly beneficial hormone-like effects on the body. Tofu - and soya products generally - contain a specific family of phytoestrogens known as "isoflavones" which help to reduce the risk of osteoporosis, menopausal symptoms, diabetes, heart disease, and many other chronic diseases. Because of its anti-inflammatory properties, it is equally suitable for men and for women.

Because of their weak oestrogenic effect in the body, phytoestrogens can either take up oestrogen receptor sites and help to lower levels of oestrogen which are too high; or, where oestrogen levels are too low, these will be gently increased. One of the major problems for men to-day is the fact that the environment is so full of "Xeno" oestrogens - compounds which mimic oestrogen and are derived from pesticides, household chemicals and many types of plastics - that their testosterone levels are becoming lower. Here again, tofu is at least part of the answer.

Tofu is also rich in the B vitamins and in iron. Sometimes it is prepared with calcium sulphate, which adds to its calcium content.

It is no coincidence that, in the countries where tofu and other soya products such as miso, tempeh, soya sauce, TVP (textured soya protein) and soya milk are eaten on a daily basis, incidence of cancer, menopausal symptoms and osteoporosis is much lower than countries which depend more heavily on dairy products.

Some women even find that they are able to come off, or avoid the necessity of, HRT - particularly if combined with daily consumption of 1-2 tablespoons of freshly ground flax or linseeds.

Tofu blend (1) *(tastes really naughty but is delicious AND healthy!)*

Into a blender, place:
half a block of tofu,   A banana
Sufficient soya milk to cover   1 tbsp. olive oil or lecithin granules

Blend until *really* creamy. Add a little fructose if you feel you want something sweeter.

To make it really special, add 1 tbsp Black and Green's Organic Cocoa.

Tofu blend (2)

Into a blender, place:
half a block of tofu   1 tbsp. olive oil or lecithin granules
1 small tin of fruit in own juice (pineapple, prunes, raspberries etc.)

Blend until *really* creamy. This version should not need the fructose added.
For a party pudding, try adding a spoonful of brandy, Kirsch, or Grand Marnier.

Soya shake

100 grams /4 oz fresh fruit

1 tbsp fruit concentrate

4 tbsp Yofu

4 tbsp soya ice cream

Liquidize until really smooth, adding water to required consistency.

Tofu mayonnaise - *use in place of normal mayonnaise*

7 oz/200g mashed tofu

¼ tsp. dried mustard

1-3 tbsp. cider vinegar or lemon juice according to taste

8 tbsp. olive oil

Sea salt to taste.

Put all ingredients into a blender and mix until really smooth.

Tofu dressing - *delicious on baked potato or sweet potato*

Half a block of tofu

Soya milk to make a creamy consistency

Lemon juice to taste

1 tbsp. olive oil

Sea salt to taste

Blend until creamy and use either plain or with the addition of chives or mixed herbs

Tofu cottage cheese

7-8oz/200g tofu, drained and pressed

2-3 tbsp. yogurt, crème fraiche or soured cream

Sea salt to taste

Mix the ingredients using a fork until the desired consistency is achieved. Add chives or chopped pineapple.

Tofu cream cheese

10 oz/300g drained and pressed tofu
2 tbsp. olive oil
sea salt to taste

Combine all ingredients in a blender and mix until smooth. If it becomes too stiff, add either soya milk or more olive oil depending on the texture you prefer. Good for stuffing sticks of celery or dates!

Tofu in Soup

Any homemade soup can be converted into a "cream" soup with the addition of a good chunk of tofu. This has the twin benefits of adding to its protein content and giving it the creamy texture normally only obtained by adding cream.

Creamy tomato soup

1 onion, chopped
1 tin of tomatoes
1 carrot
1 stick of celery
1 tbsp olive oil
1 litre / 1 ¾ pints stock or water
100 g/4 oz tofu
Sea salt and freshly ground pepper

Gently fry the onion, carrot and celery in the olive oil. Add the tomatoes and stock or water. Simmer until the vegetables are tender (15-20 minutes). Add the tofu and liquidize. Season to taste.

Sauces and stir-fries

This is where the bland nature of tofu comes in so useful as it takes on the flavour of any well-flavoured sauce or vegetables. If it is still too bland for your taste, add tamari or soya sauce to perk it up a bit.

Tofu, tuna and anchovy dressing

Half a block of tofu
1 tin tuna in olive oil
1 tin anchovies (omit if you don't like them)

Empty the contents of the tins of fish into a blender; add the mashed tofu, and blend thoroughly. Add a little soya milk or hot water if it is too thick to blend. A little fresh lemon juice can also be added.

Chocolate frozen pudding

10 ½ oz/300g tofu
3 tbsp. olive oil
4 tbsp. Black & Green's organic cocoa

Pinch of salt
1 tsp. vanilla essence
3 oz brown or molasses sugar

Mix all ingredients in blender. Spoon into a bowl or freezer container, cover and freeze for about four hours or until the mixture is mushy. If leaving in the freezer for longer, it is best thawed slightly at room temperature for about half an hour.

Carob pudding

½ pint/10 fl oz soya milk
4 tbsp carob powder (or you could use Black & Green's Cocoa powder)
2 tsp vanilla essence

75g/3oz sunflower seeds
1 tbsp olive oil
75g/3oz pitted dates

Place all ingredients into a liquidizer and blend until thoroughly creamy.

Tofu lemon dessert

10 fl oz/½ pint water
Juice of 1 ½ lemons
1 egg white

200g/7 oz mashed tofu
3 tbsp. gelatine soaked in 3 tbsp. water
4 tbsp. brown or muscavado sugar

In a saucepan, combine the water and sugar. Heat until the sugar has dissolved. Add the soaked gelatine and dissolve, without boiling, over a low heat. Add the lemon juice, mix and allow to cool. Add the tofu and blend. Beat the egg white and fold into the mixture. Put into a dish or mould and chill.

This is delicious served with a raspberry sauce made by pureeing 7 oz ripe raspberries and adding sugar to taste.

Tofu creamy topping

12 oz/350g drained tofu
Light muscavado sugar to taste

1 tsp. vanilla essence
1 tbsp. olive oil

Mix all the ingredients in a blender to taste. Use as whipped cream and keep any surplus in the fridge (covered). For a thinner "cream", add soya milk to the required consistency.

Tofu and spinach cannelloni

For convenience use cannelloni which does not require pre-cooking.

Allow 2 cannelloni "tubes" per person
7oz/200 g frozen, chopped spinach
1 tbsp olive oil
fresh or dried basil
a little grated parmesan cheese.

7oz/200g tofu
1 onion
1 tin chopped tomatoes
salt and freshly ground pepper

Cook the frozen spinach and drain well. Allow to cool. Meanwhile, make a tomato sauce by heating the olive oil and cooking the chopped onion until soft. Then add the contents of the tin of tomato and simmer for about 5 minutes. Add the basil. Mash the tofu with a fork and mix in the cooked spinach. Fill the cannelloni tubes. Place in an ovenware dish and cover with tomato sauce. Cook in a moderate oven for the length of time specified on the packet of cannelloni usually about 20-30 minutes, but different makes vary. Scatter Parmesan cheese on top before serving.

Tofu dressing (2)

75g/3oz tofu
1 tsp wholegrain mustard
8 basil leaves
1 tsp bouillon powder
4 tbsp water

Place all ingredients into a liquidizer and whiz until thoroughly blended. Serve with baked potato and/or salad.

Apricot cream

8 oz/225g unsulphured apricots, soaked overnight
12oz/350g Silken Tofu
A little lemon juice
2 pieces of chopped stem ginger (optional)

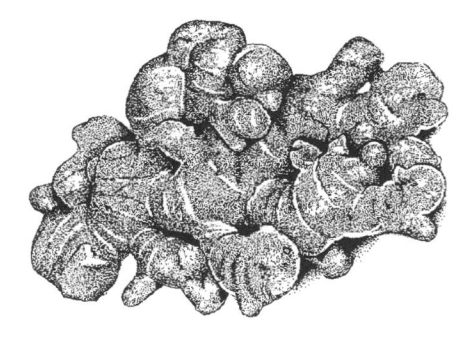

Place the tofu, lemon juice and apricots in a blender with sufficient juice to liquidize until really smooth and creamy. Sprinkle with toasted almonds or hazelnuts.

Banana dream

2 ripe bananas
10fl oz (300ml) soya milk
4 oz (100ml) tofu
1 tbsp hazelnut oil

Blend in liquidizer until thoroughly creamy. Pour into glasses. Grate a square of dark (70% cocoa solids) chocolate over the top of each glass.

There are so many different combinations of fruit and tofu which blend to make a wonderfully healthy pudding. The addition of a tablespoon of olive or cold-pressed nut oil, or lecithin has the effect of giving it a creamier consistency. Experiment and enjoy!

Orange cream

8 oz/225g Silken tofu

2 tbsp concentrated orange juice

1 tbsp Grand Marnier (optional)

1 tsp fresh lemon juice

Blend all the ingredients and pour into serving glasses. Decorate each with an orange section

This can also be made with stoned cherries and optional Kirsch;　or with prunes and optional brandy.

The Big Breakfast 7

The Big Breakfast

Why breakfast?

We have all heard the expression "breakfast like a king; lunch like a lord, dine like a pauper". For most of us these days, this way of eating is neither feasible nor desirable, but the fact is that we seem to have completely reversed the order, and with detrimental effects. So often, we either don't have time for breakfast, or eat it while on the hoof and doing numerous other things. Some people find they simply can't face eating until later in the morning, or even until lunch-time, and yet others go all day without a proper meal and then eat massive amounts in the evening only to find - surprise surprise - that they can't face breakfast again.

The main benefit of eating a good breakfast, and one which contains at least some form of protein, is that blood sugar levels are gently raised, and sustained until lunch-time. When you skip breakfast, you will often find that you have the classical "4 o'clock dip" in your energy levels. Raising blood sugar levels might sound like an excellent excuse for a coffee and doughnut, but the fact is that such foods raise the levels much too quickly and, because they contain nothing which will sustain that rise, they come crashing down again within an hour or so. This is where the cravings and "must have's" kick in and of course, the easiest option is more coffee and a biscuit. After a day of this roller-coaster effect, it's no wonder that energy levels are at an all-time low around 4 o'clock, or that all you really want to do when you get home is slump into a chair and eat …..yes, convenience food.

There is no doubt that some people really do feel better if they just have fruit for breakfast, and that seems to get them through to lunch-time quite happily. In fact, when trying to persuade people to start to have at least something in the morning, a piece or two of fresh fruit is often the best way to do so.

Mornings are, for some people, undoubtedly frantic, and may seem even more so if you are more of an "owl" than a "lark". "Owls" could spend a little time last thing at night preparing something simple for the morning - either to eat at home, or to take to work. I sometimes need to be on a 6.30 am train, so a blender breakfast prepared the night before and kept in the fridge until it's time to run, is a Godsend (don't forget to take a spoon!). Some fresh fruit and a bag of mixed seeds and nuts fill the bill just as well.

For those of you who really feel you need a slice of toast, do ensure that it contains the whole grain - rye, spelt or wheat - as the protein content is higher and the fibre helps to keep blood sugar levels balanced. Some tahini (sesame seed) spread, cottage cheese, almond or sugar-free peanut butter will increase the protein content of the meal.

If you're having fruit juice as part of breakfast, you may find that it is better to drink this about 20 minutes beforehand so that it does not interfere with carbohydrate digestion.

A note on muesli

When Dr. Bircher Benner, a Swiss physician, invented his muesli, he did so because his patients needed a food which was easily digested and assimilated. His recipe was for 1-2 tablespoons of oats (nowadays we should aim for organic quality), which were soaked overnight in milk or water. This allowed for the complete expansion of the oats, and for this same reason you could also put in any dried fruits you wish to add at the same time. In the morning, freshly sliced fruit was added and some milled almonds or hazelnuts. I often think that if Dr. Benner were to see some of the products on the supermarket shelves which pass for "muesli" he would turn in his grave. The recipes we give are based more on the original muesli so will taste quite different to the commercial variety. Should you feel the need to add extra fibre, we recommend the use of oat, rice or soya bran rather than wheat bran which is too harsh for most people's systems.

Blender breakfasts

The advantage of these is that they can be made the night before; can contain any of a variety of ingredients; can be put into a container and transported if necessary; and - should you have made more than you want to have for breakfast - double up as a healthy "pudding" or snack for later in the day. You can also add any nutritional supplements you may be taking, either ground up if they are in tablet form, or by emptying the contents of a capsule unless the instructions on the box say you should not do so.

For example, into a blender put the following ingredients:

> ¼-½ pint (150-300mls) diluted fruit juice, soya milk, oat milk, Rice Dream, or animal milk if tolerated
> 1 banana or other soft fruit (prunes, apricots, raspberries, strawberries etc.)
> 1 tbsp ground sunflower or sesame seeds; hazelnuts or almonds (for Omega 6 fatty acids)
> 1 tbsp ground pumpkin or linseeds; or walnuts (for Omega 3 fatty acids)

Ideally the seeds or nuts should be ground freshly each day, but you could do enough for 2-3 days if they're put into a screw-topped container in the fridge. A coffee grinder is perfect for this job.

Liquidize until really smooth and creamy. The consistency may be varied according to taste - simply add more water to thin. Sip slowly or eat with a spoon. The contents of any vitamin or mineral capsules may also be added to the mixture.

By using this combination of nuts and seeds, it ensures a balanced intake of the essential fatty acids, and a good supply of vitamins and minerals particularly calcium, magnesium and zinc.

Tofu smoothie

Put 6oz/150g tofu into the blender with sufficient milk or soya milk to make a creamy consistency. Add a banana or other fresh fruit in season, or 4-5 previously soaked prunes and blend to required consistency.

Alternatively, put 6oz/150g tofu into the blender with a tin of fruit in its own juice and liquidize until it becomes the required consistency (i.e. smooth or with pieces of fruit according to taste).

Avocado smoothie

Liquidize an avocado with ¾ pint/425ml soya, oat or rice milk, a small banana and a handful of any fresh fruit in season. Serves 2.

Fruit compote with yoghurt

Fold 4 tbsp sheep's or goat's yogurt into a generous helping of apple of mixed fruit compote. Sprinkle with toasted chopped almonds or sunflower seeds.

The Energy Breakfast

Soak 2 tbsp oat, brown rice or millet flakes - or a mixture - overnight in milk, milk alternatives or diluted fruit juice. Add 2 tbsp ground mixed seeds - a mixture of sunflower, sesame, pumpkin and linseeds - and more liquid if required. You may prefer the seeds to be whole; they just require more chewing! Top with a chopped banana or other fresh fruit. If you really need to make it sweeter, a small amount of fructose or fructo-oligosaccharides (FOS) may also be added.

FOS are naturally occurring sugars which help to maintain a healthy intestinal flora and give a "lift" to breakfast. They are obtainable at a good Health Food Shop.

Mega Muesli

4 cups organic jumbo oats	½ cup dried apricots
2 cups organic cornflakes	½ cup sunflower seeds
2 cups organic millet flakes	½ cup pumpkin seeds
½ cup almonds	½ cup walnuts
½ cup coconut (optional)	½ cup crystallized ginger (optional but delicious)

Mix together in a large plastic container and keep in the fridge.

This muesli is best soaked in milk, soya or rice milk, or diluted fruit juice, for an hour or so before eating. Top with seedless grapes or other fresh fruit and a tablespoon of organic yoghurt or Yofu.

Summer muesli

Soak porridge or jumbo oats overnight in skimmed milk, or soya milk and water. In the morning, add fresh berry fruits or nectarines, and a tbsp or so of fresh, live, yoghurt.

Porridge

Make with organic oats - jumbo or standard, and milk/soya milk and water. Top with 2 tbsp of mixed seeds or nuts and a little fresh or dried fruit.

Rice porridge

Made as above but using brown rice flakes (see page 37).

Breakfast on the hoof

Basically, this is never a good idea, but we can't be perfect all the time! My emergency breakfast for eating in the car or on the train consists of a couple of pieces of fresh fruit and about 2 tbsp mixed seeds and/or nuts.

Other breakfast ideas

- Plain, live ("bio") yoghurt, with added seeds, nuts, wheat germ and/or fruit.

- Millet or brown rice flake porridge. This is made in the same way as "normal" porridge, although I prefer to soak the flakes overnight to cut down on cooking time in the morning. Dried fruit or chopped banana can be stirred in towards the end of the cooking time, and seeds sprinkled on top.

- Eggs - poached, boiled, scrambled, omelette.

- Tinned fruit in own juice with ground or whole seeds/nuts.

- Wholemeal or rye toast with a little *butter or non-hydrogenated* margarine and crunchy peanut butter, cottage cheese or almond butter. Top with sliced apple.

- Kippers, grilled or put in a saucepan of just-boiled water or about five minutes.

A note on drinks

As the drinks such as tea and coffee act as stimulants and play havoc with blood sugar levels, it is best to limit your intake quite severely. We would recommend having one cup of really good, fresh, coffee or tea if you don't wish to give them up entirely, or substitute with coffee alternatives such as Caro Extra, Barley Cup, Bambu, No-Caff; Rooibosch tea (which contains neither caffeine nor tannin and is the nearest to "real" tea); or herb teas. In reply to the frequently asked question "what about de-caffeinated coffee?" the answer is that this contains other, potentially harmful, chemicals known as xanthines, not to mention the chemicals which have been used in some types of decaffeination process. Some people find a glass of hot water with a slice of lemon taken before breakfast to be beneficial.

The only true drink is water - filtered or bottled. 1-1½ litres per day should be your aim.

Adding a little fruit juice for flavour may encourage you to drink more.

Squeezing The Last Ounce

8

If you already have a juicer, you will know what a delicious and easy method this is by which to obtain your daily 5-7 portions of fruit and vegetables per day. Children who refuse to eat vegetables at all or only a very limited variety, will usually down them with gusto if they have been juiced.

Juicers come in two main types and as with all such equipment, it is worth getting the best you can afford. The centrifugal type incorporates a fine-meshed basket which can get a bit clogged up and tends not to extract "the last ounce". It is, however, cheaper. The masticating type of juicer chews the fibres and breaks up the cells of vegetables and fruits, thereby adding some fibre as well as ensuring total availability of all enzymes, vitamins and minerals. Pulp from the first juicing can be re-fed into the juicer two or three times. It is, however, considerably more expensive. Both types are relatively easy to clean.

Because juices are quickly assimilated, they are an excellent way of boosting energy levels. Ideally, they should be taken 20 minutes before a meal, or as a snack any time during the day. They come complete with their own digestive enzymes, thereby making them highly beneficial to anyone with poor digestion, the elderly, or anyone not feeling well enough to cope with a full meal.

Ideally, organic produce should be used and this will only require washing. Non-organic produce should be peeled. Any damaged portions should be removed, as well as fruit stones. The seeds of fruits such as grapes, melons, apples, oranges, lemons and grapefruit, may be included. The white pith found on citrus fruits may also be included as it is a valuable source of Vitamin C and the bioflavonoids which aid its absorption and act as powerful anti-oxidants. With vegetable juices, leaves and stems which would not normally be eaten can be added to the juice.

Try to use fruits and vegetables in season, and fruit should be as ripe as possible.

Melon cooler

If the melon is organic, scrub the skin and cut into strips. Juice the whole fruit including seeds and skin! Otherwise, peel, but include seeds.

Pineapple juice

Scrub the skin, chop into strips and feed the whole fruit through. This gives a thick juice to be sipped - strain if you prefer a clear juice.

Mixed fruit juices

Most fruits in season combine well and your choice will mainly depend on what is easily and cheaply available. Generally speaking it is best not to use more than three or four different varieties. Try combinations of the following:

Apples	apricots
Bilberries (blueberries)	cherries
Grapefruit	grapes
Mangoes	melon (all types)
nectarines	oranges
Peaches	pears
Pineapple	strawberries

Tomato juice

This is an excellent way of using very (but not over) ripe tomatoes.

Juice the tomatoes and season to taste. The addition of celery gives a tasty juice. A quick and easy appetizer.

Carrot juice

This is a good vegetable juice to start with and children love it. Always use fresh, crisp carrots and make sure you cut off the top ¼ inch. Scrub organic carrots; peel non-organic ones. 2lb/900g carrots will make approximately 1 pint/600mls of juice

Mixed vegetable juice

The permutations here are endless and will depend upon availability and the time of year. It's a good idea to use carrots as a base, as they give a certain amount of sweetness. The following are just a few suggestions for adding in:

beetroot	celery
spinach*	parsley
sweet potatoes	tomatoes
cucumber	broccoli
red, green and yellow peppers	kale*
cauliflower*	watercress
fennel	lettuce leaves*
courgettes	beansprouts

*These can be a bit bitter, so go easy to begin with.

Generally speaking it is best not to combine fruit and vegetables, although the addition of an apple can often take away any bitterness.

For extra flavour add a clove of garlic, or a slice of fresh ginger.

Cleansing cocktail

¼ "/5mm slice ginger root   1 beetroot
½ apple, seeded   4 carrots

Push all ingredients through hopper and drink immediately.

Ginger fizz

¼"/5mm slice ginger root   1 apple, de-seeded
Sparkling water

Push ginger through hopper with the apple. Pour juice into a glass and top with sparkling water.

Low-sugar pop

1 apple, de-seeded   ¼ lime
Sparkling water

Juice apple and lime. Pour into a tall glass and top up with sparkling water.

Ginger ale

1 lemon wedge   ¼ "/5mm slice ginger root
1 medium bunch green grapes   Sparkling water

Juice the lemon. Push the ginger through the hopper with the grapes. Pour the juice into a tall glass and top with sparkling water.

Immune booster

2 carrots, scrubbed
1 apple
2 cloves garlic
½ lemon, peeled.

1 beetroot
a handful of spinach
2 sprigs garlic

Feed all the ingredients through the hopper, cutting if required.   Serve immediately.

Blackberry and apple zinger

2 eating apples
a handful of blackberries
a knob of ginger, peeled (optional)

Put the blackberries in the machine first and push through with the quartered or sliced. Apple.

This can also be made with raspberries, strawberries or blueberries.

Calcium-rich cocktail

This is excellent if you are on a dairy-free diet and worried about calcium intake.
4-5 carrots, scrubbed
1 apple
3 kale leaves
Small handful of parsley.

Bunch up the kale and parsley and push through the hopper with the carrots and apple.

The Portable Lunch - not a sarnie in sight

For most people going out to work, lunch is the most difficult meal of the day. It is so easy either to "just grab a sandwich"; stop at a garage or local store for a block of chocolate; or simply do without. Those working at home sometimes fare little better as they raid the biscuit tin or fill up on all the wrong things.

Although most of us cope very well with the occasional - preferably wholemeal - sandwich, the majority of people feel better when they severely curtail their wheat consumption. Wheat is hard to digest and is responsible for many a bloated stomach! It can slow down the metabolism, and block the uptake of essential nutrients. It can also make you feel very sleepy after lunch; this may be due to the fact that certain components of wheat compete with the body's endorphins, which are vital brain chemicals involved in mood elevation. For this reason, we have concentrated on foods which are vital and energizing.

The portable lunch really does have to be thought about the night before. For example, if you are cooking rice for supper, an extra couple of ounces will provide the basis for a rice salad. You can do the same thing with potatoes, millet, quinoa, green or Puy lentils or pasta. Although our recipe for a nut loaf might make a little time to make, it takes very little longer to make two. What is left over from a meal can then be sliced, individually wrapped, and frozen. With the addition of a large salad and perhaps a piece of fruit, you have a healthy and balanced meal.

On really difficult days, two pieces of fruit and a small bag of fresh nuts and seeds fill the lunch-time gap very well.

It is useful to keep a tin of oatcakes, ricecakes or Ryvita at your place of work. If you have the use of a fridge, a large box of cottage cheese, tofu "cheese", hummus, almond or sugar-free peanut butter can be kept there, together with a large bag of mixed salad and some tomatoes. Smoked tofu and smoked mackerel, salmon or trout are useful sources of protein.

Once you get the hang of making meal-sized soups, the quantities can easily be doubled up with the remainder put into containers in the freezer and then reheated and taken to work in a thermos flask. Some flasks have different sections so that all sorts of components of last night's meal can be used for lunch.

Tins of fish (in a well ventilated room!) and boiled eggs are excellent convenience meals, as are avocado pears.

Nutty lentil paté

8 oz (225g) red lentils
2 tbsp olive oil
1-2 tsp mixed herbs
Seasoning to taste.

1 medium onion, finely chopped
¾ pint (420mls) vegetable stock
3 oz (75g) walnut pieces

Heat the oil and gently sauté the onion. Add the lentils and cook a minute longer. Pour in the stock, seasoning and herbs. Bring to the boil and simmer until all the water has been absorbed. Set aside to cool. Meanwhile, grind the walnuts. Mash the lentils, or put into a food processor; add the nuts and turn into a serving dish. Divide into portions and freeze until required. Pile on to oat or rice cakes, pumpernickel or Ryvita.

Tofu, tuna and anchovy paté

Half a block of tofu
1 tin tuna in olive oil
1 tin anchovies (omit if you don't like them)

Empty the contents of the tins of fish into a blender; add the mashed tofu and blend thoroughly. (Add a little soya milk or hot water if the mixture is too thick for your blender.) A little fresh lemon juice and some parsley can also be added.

Celery, yoghurt and date salad

1 head of celery
6 oz/150g dates
1/3 pint/150g plain, live yoghurt
sunflower seeds

Discard any tough celery stalks (save for soup); slice the rest finely, then mixed with yoghurt and chopped dates. Add a few sunflower (or pumpkin) seeds.

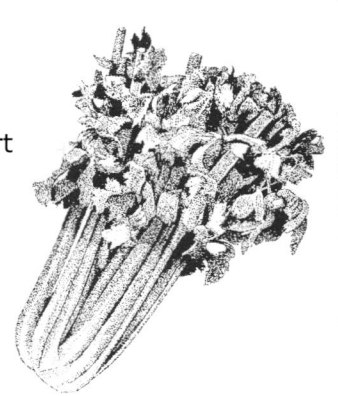

Avocado paté salad

1 avocado pear
juice of ½ lemon
drop of Tabasco
lettuce, watercress, tomato
8 oz/225grams cottage cheese
paprika

Halve, stone and peel avocado. Mash it into the lemon juice and cottage cheese, season with one drop of Tabasco. Arrange on lettuce, decorate with watercress and tomato, dust with paprika.

Fruit salad with cottage cheese dressing

2 pieces of fresh fruit in season
A few grapes
Lettuce
4 oz /100g cottage cheese
1 tbsp plain yoghurt, milk or soya milk
a few chopped nuts

Wash and slice fruits. Thin cottage cheese with milk or yoghurt. Spoon creamy cottage cheese mixture over the fruit. Top with chopped nuts - fresh or lightly toasted.

Pineapple and tofutti (tofu "cream cheese") salad

4 slices pineapple
lettuce leaves
toasted flaked almonds
black grapes or strawberries
6 oz /150g Tofutti

Put lettuce leaves into lunch box; chop pineapple slices and put into box. Top with Tofutti and decorate with nuts and grapes or strawberries.

Vitamin salad

Lettuce leaves
grated cabbage
tomato
raw beetroot, grated
1 tbsp chopped dates
grated carrot
1 tbsp ground brazil nuts
sliced cucumber
French dressing.

Line lunch box with lettuce leaves; add other salad vegetables. Mix brazil nuts and dates; add to box and cover with French dressing.

Banana and nut salad

Peel banana, cut into three, then cut each piece in half lengthways. Roll in milled nuts or sesame seeds. Serve with a green salad and French Dressing.

Hummus (can be bought ready-made, but is even better when home-made)

14 oz /400 g can chickpeas
1 tbsp tahini
2 tbsp olive oil
juice of a lemon
black pepper
1 clove garlic (if you can get away with it!)

Drain chickpeas, reserving liquid. Liquidize with oil, tahini and lemon juice, adding more liquid if needed. Serve with a large salad and oat or rice cakes, or halve an avocado pear and put 1 tbsp hummus in the middle. Serve with tomato salad.

Rice salad - serve with Crunchy Peanut Dressing or Peanut & Sesame Sauce

Always cook more rice than you require for the evening meal. If all else fails, you can toss it in a French dressing, stir in some lightly toasted nuts or seeds, and have with a mixed salad. If you also happen to have some leftover peas, it becomes the Italian classic "Risi Bisi".

To make a really delicious meal, however, it is great served with either:

Crunchy peanut dressing

4 tbs olive oil
juice of a lemon

2 tbsp soya sauce
1 tbsp crunchy peanut butter

Blend all ingredients; season to taste.

Or:

Peanut and sesame sauce

1 tbsp peanut butter
1 small onion, finely chopped
1-2 tsp tamari or soya sauce

1 tbsp tahini
200-300ml/7-10fl oz diluted apple juice

Blend all ingredients together until smooth. Heat gently in a small pan, stirring constantly. The sauce will thicken as it cooks. Allow to cool before putting into lunch box.

Stuffed tomatoes

2 tomatoes	cottage cheese
chives	sea salt, paprika

Halve the tomatoes and scoop out the flesh. Mix the cottage cheese, tomato pulp and chopped chives. Sprinkle the insides of the tomato shells with salt and paprika, then pile the cheese mixture into the tomato cases. Serve on a bed of lettuce and watercress and eat with oatcakes, rice cakes, Ryvita, wholemeal or rye bread

Small chunks or flakes of tuna, left-over salmon or chicken can be mixed into the cottage cheese.

Smoked salmon paté

Put half a pound of smoked salmon trimmings in a food processor and chop briefly. Then add three tablespoons olive oil, four tablespoons of water, the juice of half a lemon and 2 tbs plain yoghurt. Process until pale and fluffy, adding more liquid if needed. Serve with salad and Ryvita or rye bread.

Avocado with smoked fish

½ ripe avocado	2 slices smoked salmon, mackerel, trout or chicken
Juice of a lemon	2 tbsp olive, walnut or pumpkin oil
Sea salt and freshly ground black pepper	

Mix the oil, lemon juice and seasoning to make a dressing. Skin and slice the avocado lengthways. Lay the slices over the smoked fish or meat, and dribble the dressing over. Serve with brown rice, new potatoes, crispbreads or wholemeal bread.

Smoked mackerel dip

9 oz/250g plain, live yoghurt or Yofu
1 large mackerel fillet (plain or peppered)
Herbs and seasoning to taste

Put the yoghurt into a blender with the mackerel chopped into pieces. Add the seasoning and herbs and blend until smooth. Serve with corn chips and fingers of carrot, celery and/or peppers.

Quorn waldorf salad

Mix chunks of quorn with a chopped up apple, a few walnuts and a chopped stick of celery. Dress with yoghurt blended with lemon juice, salt and pepper, or tofu mayonnaise (see page 62).

Carrot and celeriac slaw

Grated carrot and celeriac in equal parts in a dressing made with Greek yoghurt, a teaspoon of French mustard, a few chopped gherkins or capers and chopped chives. Scatter toasted sesame seeds on top.

Salad ideas:

Chopped Brussels Sprouts with chopped walnuts and mayonnaise.
Shredded white cabbage with Muscatel raisins, sunflower seeds and French dressing.
Cucumber, chopped and covered with natural yoghurt and sprinkled with chopped parsley.
Grated carrots and coconut with French Dressing.
Beetroot, apples and/or celery, grated, with almonds and chives or parsley.
Lentils and roasted vegetables, with a light French Dressing. Some crumbled goats cheese can also be added.

10

Slow, Slow, Quick, Quick, Slow

the slow cooker

If I were only allowed one piece of kitchen equipment apart from my conventional cooker and a fridge, it would have to be a slow cooker. Even when cooking for one, it is completely invaluable for those days when you come in starving, or have only half an hour to eat and be out again. It is even more satisfying to know that you can feed several people in that amount of time with just a little preparation in the morning.

Further advantages of the slow cooker are that the meal won't spoil if it has to be delayed even by an hour or two - and it's ideal if different members of the family need to eat at different times. Also, the flavour tends to be better than fast cooking for most dishes. It is also an excellent means of cooking a large casserole which can be divided into portions and put into the freezer for future eating.

If going out to buy a slow cooker, try to get one with two or three speeds. Cooking on High can produce lunch or dinner while you are out for a few hours, while cooking on Low, or Auto, will allow the meal to cook all day. It is so good to come home to the smell of a nutritious meal when you haven't been near the kitchen for hours! My preferred slow cooker is the Russell Hobbs Model 4436 as it has the dual control, holds 3 litres, lifts out for easy cleaning and also looks good.

If you are not familiar with this type of cooking, it is important to know that vegetables actually take longer to cook than meat. They should therefore either be sliced or chopped finely, or they should be sautéed for a few minutes. It's a good idea to put them on the bottom of the cooker, with the exception of potatoes which can be layered on top. Another difference between slow and conventional cooking is that you will need less liquid as evaporation is very slight. Gentle heat tends to make the cheaper cuts of meat more tender, and a joint will shrink less as it retains its moisture.

Because a Slow Cooker uses only slightly more electricity than a light bulb, it is an ideal way for those on a budget to cook the cheaper cuts of meat and pulses which would normally use up greater amounts of fuel. Also, because it heats the food and not the kitchen, that feeling of "slaving over a hot stove" can be avoided.

I definitely find that flavours are improved when pre-browned in a little olive oil in a frying or saucepan, but if time does not permit, many recipes will be perfectly acceptable if the ingredients are placed into the cooker directly. It should, however, be pre-warmed for 20 minutes, and any liquid which is added should be boiling. n order to thicken gravy or sauce, meat can either be rolled in flour as for normal braising, or 1-2 tbs flour can be blended with a little stock and added to the casserole 30 minutes before serving.

In addition to the recipes which follow, I also find the cooker useful for making stock overnight with bones which are left over from the previous meal - a welcome addition to any home-made soup - or any variety of tasty soups can be left simmering all day or all night. Put some well-scrubbed, medium-sized potatoes into the Cooker before you leave for work in the morning, and they will be ready to have with your favourite filling, or baked beans, and a salad shortly after arriving home (8-10 hours). You can also use this method for cooking potatoes for a barbecue; talking of which, you could also have a tasty sauce simmering and ready for dressing different types of kebab.

Stuffed vegetables - peppers, marrow, butternut squash and aubergines - do really well and can be served with a quick tomato sauce (see "Dressing for Dinner"). The sauce can either be poured around the vegetables, or made and served separately.

Porridge lovers can awake to a bowl of ready-to-go porridge by putting one cup of oatmeal to about 3 cups of water (or milk and water) plus a pinch of salt into the Slow Cooker last thing at night. Cover and cook on Low for 8-9 hours. Serve with milk, soya milk or plain, live yogurt. For a more substantial breakfast add half a chopped banana and a tbs of mixed seeds.

SOUPS

Chicken or meat broth

350g (12oz) lean chicken, beef or lamb pieces
175g (6oz) finely chopped swede
1 litre (2 pints) water
175g (6oz) thinly sliced leeks
50g (2 oz) pearl barley
Sea salt and freshly ground pepper to taste
2 onions, finely chopped
Herbs and garlic (optional)
175g (6oz) finely chopped carrots

Put the meat into a pan and cover with cold water. Bring to the boil. Remove any scum. Add all other ingredients and bring to the boil again. Transfer to the Slow cooker and cook on High for 4-6 hours (8-12 hours on Low/Auto).

Vegetable soup

Lightly sauté about 1kg (2 lb) mixed vegetables according to availability. Stir in 25g/1 oz flour or rice flour and add 900mls (1½ pints) stock or water with 2 tsp stock powder. Bring to the boil, season and transfer to Slow Cooker. Cook on High for 4-6 hours (6-12 hours on Low/Auto).

Pea soup

250g (8oz) split green peas
1 carrot
1 bay leaf
Sea salt and freshly ground black pepper
1 litre (1¾ pints) well-flavoured stock
1 stalk celery
Fresh parsley to decorate
Crème fraiche

Soak the peas overnight in plenty of water. Drain. Place in the Slow Cooker with the stock, chopped celery and carrot. Cover and cook on Low/Auto for 8-10 hours. Liquidize and season to taste. Decorate with a swirl of crème fraiche and decorate with chopped parsley.

Curried lentil soup

250g (8oz) green or brown lentils
2 tsp curry powder (vary according to taste)
1 clove garlic
1 stalk celery, chopped
900ml (1 ½ pints) stock or water
1 tbsp ghee or olive oil
1 onion, chopped
1 carrot, diced
Sea salt an black pepper to taste

Wash the lentils and put into the Slow Cooker with the stock or water. Warm the ghee/oil in a saucepan, add the curry powder, onion, garlic, carrot and celery. Cook gently for 5 minutes. Add to the lentils. Cover and cook on Low/Auto for 8-10 hours. Season to taste. May either be liquidized for a smooth texture, or served whole.

CURRIES cook really well in the Slow Cooker and it is quite easy to adapt a favourite recipe to this type of cooking. The following recipe is from Russell Hobbs and is a good basic recipe:

60mls (4tbsp) ghee (or olive oil)	2 onions, chopped
1 clove garlic, crushed	2.5ml (½ tsp) chilli
2.5ml (½tsp) Turmeric	2.5ml (½ tsp) Coriander
2.5ml (½ tsp) Cumin	8 oz (225g) lentils
900ml (1 ½ pts) stock	5 ml (1 tsp) lemon juice
Sea Salt and freshly ground pepper to taste	2 carrots, diced
1 apple, peeled, cored and chopped	50g (2oz) sultanas.

Heat the ghee or oil in a pan. Sauté the onion and the garlic lightly. Add the chilli, turmeric, coriander, cumin and lentils. Cook gently for one minute. Stir in the stock, lemon juice, salt and pepper. Bring to the boil and continue to boil for five minutes. Transfer to the Slow Cooker and stir in the carrots, apple and sultanas. Cook for 3-4 hours on High (Low/Auto 7-10 hours).

If you prefer to use meat, this should be lightly sautéed before the onion and placed in the Slow Cooker.

FISH

Most types of fish benefit from being cooked in the Slow cooker as their delicate flavours are effectively retained. Another advantage is that the fish holds together vary well, although it is important as - with all fish cookery - not to cook it for too long. Many people are put off fish by the preparation it needs, so don't forget to ask the fishmonger to do so for you. The other main objection is the smell! Putting it in the slow cooker will avoid this.

General Method

1. Grease the base of the cooking pot with butter or olive oil.
2. Clean, trim and wash the fish (rolled fillets and steaks are most suitable). Frozen fish should be completely thawed before slow cooking. Dry and place in the Slow Cooker.
3. Season to taste, sprinkle with lemon juice then add a little hot stock, water or wine.
4. Dot some butter over the fish if desired
5. Cook on auto for approximately 2 hours.

The following recipe is a really easy one to get started on:

Poached salmon cutlets

(For 4 people)

4 x 175g-225g (6oz-8oz) salmon cutlets
150ml/¼ pint white wine
1 bay leaf
1 onion, thinly sliced

300ml/½ pint water
2.5ml/½ tsp sea salt
2 pepper corns
1 sprig parsley

Put each salmon cutlet onto a piece of baking parchment cut to size and lower into the cooking pot. Put the remaining ingredients into a saucepan, bring to the boil and pour over the salmon. Replace the lid and cook for the about two hours on Low/Auto. Serve immediately or leave to cool in the liquid and eat cold with salad.

Fish provencal

1 piece of haddock, halibut, cod or coley per person
1 tin chopped tomatoes with onions
Sea salt and freshly ground pepper
A pinch of herbs
A few black olives (optional)

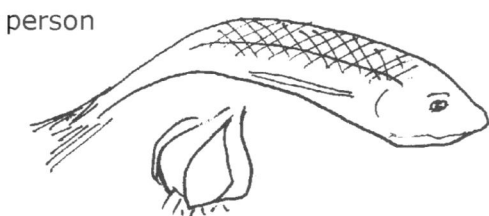

Butter the base of the cooking pot. And place the fish on top (fillets of fish can be rolled). Heat the tomatoes and onions and put over the fish. Cook on Low/Auto for about 3 hours.

Smoked haddock

500g (1lb) non-coloured smoked haddock
Freshly ground black pepper
A little butter.

4 fl oz (125ml) water
4 fl oz (125ml) milk or soya milk

Lightly butter the cooker; place smoked haddock in portion-sized pieces; cover with the milk and water. Replace lid and cook on Low/Auto for 6-8 hours, or High for 1½ - 2 hours.

If you like poached eggs with your haddock, these can be placed in the milk (around the sides of the cooker) about 20 minutes before serving.

Excellent on a bed of spinach.

MEAT

Most types of meat benefit from long, slow cooking, but it is the cheaper cuts which really come into their own in the Slow Cooker. They often have a lot more flavour than the more expensive ones and are high in nutritional value

Roasting your meat

Season the meat. In a heated frying pan, brown the meat on all sides in a little olive oil.
Transfer to the Slow Cooker and cook on High for the recommended time.
Pork joints with rind may be grilled for 10 minutes to crisp.
Turn joints once during cooking if possible to ensure even tenderness.

Weight of joint: 1-1.6Kg (2-3½ lb). Setting High   Time 5-7 hours

Braising your meat

1.5 Kg (3lb) joint of your choice
1 large onion, chopped
1 small swede, finely chopped (optional)
300ml (½pint) stock
Flour or arrowroot to thicken

1 tbsp olive oil
1 large carrot, finely chopped
1 large leek, finely sliced (optional)
1 bay leaf
Sea salt and freshly ground black pepper to taste

Heat the oil in a large pan and brown the meat well on all sides. Transfer to the Slow Cooker. In the remaining oil, fry the onions, carrots and any other vegetables used until the onion is transparent. Add the stock and bay leaf and bring to the boil. Pour round the meat. Cook on High for 6-8 hours (Low/Auto 8-10 hours). Remove the meat and place on a serving dish. Keep hot. Strain the stock. In a saucepan blend 1 tbsp flour, or rice flour, with cold water to make a paste. Gradually add the stock. Bring to the boil stirring all the time. Check seasoning.

Traditional cassoulet

4 lamb chump chops (or 450g/1lb) stewing lamb
1 smoked sausage ring, sliced
1 tbsp olive oil
1 tin of tomatoes
mixed herbs, including 2 bay leaves

2 medium sized onions
2 cloves garlic
1-2 tins of haricot beans
900ml (1 ½ pints) stock or water

Using a frying pan, gently brown the chops or stewing lamb in the oil. Transfer to the pre-heated Slow Cooker. Sauté the onions until transparent, and the garlic. Add the sausage, tomatoes, beans, stock or water and herbs. Bring to the boil and add to the cooking pot. Cook on Auto/Slow for 6-8 hours. Remove bay leaves before serving.

Bolognese sauce

If you have a family that is hooked on pasta - or baked potatoes - why not make a really large quantity of this popular sauce and freeze down into portions ready for a meal at the double? The recipe is for four servings, but you could make double or treble the amount in more or less the same amount of time.

15mls (1tbs) olive oil
2 small or 1 large onion, finely chopped
1 clove garlic, crushed
700g (1½ lb) lean and preferably organic beef
1 x 396g (14 oz) can chopped tomatoes
300ml (½ pt) stock
100g (4oz) mushrooms
1 carrot, finely diced (optional)
1 red or green pepper, chopped (optional)
1 bay leaf
1 tsp mixed herbs

Heat the oil in a pan. Add the onion and garlic and fry lightly. Add the beef and continue to fry until golden brown. Stir in the remaining ingredients and bring to the boil. Transfer to the Slow Cooker and cook for 3-4 hours on High (Low/Auto 6-8 hours). Remove the bay leaf. Serve with pasta or baked potatoes, topped with freshly grated parmesan cheese and a green salad.

Chop supper

Brown one chop per person and place in bottom of slow cooker. Sauté a selection of vegetables (carrots, onions, swede, French beans etc). Add a little stock or red wine. Top with a layer of sliced potatoes and dot with a little butter or olive oil. Cook on High for 4-6 hours (Low/Auto 6-8 hours)

Braised liver and onions

2 tbsp olive oil
450g (1 lb) organically reared lamb's liver, thinly sliced
1 rounded tbsp flour
2 large onions, thinly sliced
Sea salt and freshly ground pepper to taste
2 bay leaves
400 ml (¾pt) stock

Heat the oil in a frying pan. Coat the liver in the flour and fry gently until sealed. Transfer to the Slow Cooker. Add the onions to the pan and fry until golden. Stir in any remaining flour and the stock. Continue to stir and bring to the boil. Pour over the liver and cook on High for 2-4 hours (Low/Auto 3 ½-6 hours.)

POULTRY

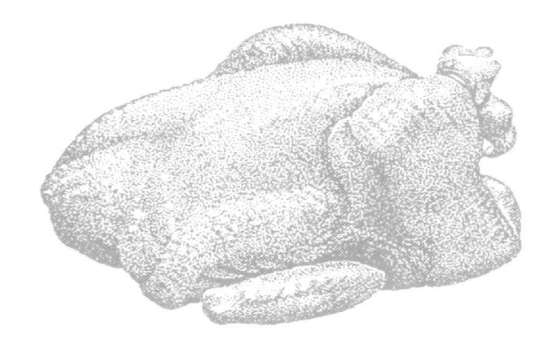

The Slow cooker is a really excellent way to cook chicken and turkey, as they are able to cook thoroughly without drying out. Chickens up to 1½ Kg (3lb) can be cooked whole; birds which are larger need to be jointed. Turkey thighs and escalopes also make tasty slowly cooked meals. Wherever possible use organically reared birds which have far more flavour and a different texture to the somewhat anaemic-looking factory farmed variety.

If cooking a duck, which tends to be very fatty, drain off the fat and discard

General method for roasting in the slow cooker

1. Wash and dry the poultry. Season lightly and, if available, put a handful of fresh herbs inside.
2. Brown the bird on all sides - either in its own fat or in a little olive oil
3. Transfer to the Slow Cooker and, for a 1½kg (3lb) bird, allow 3 ½-4 hours on high for optimum cooking time, although the meal will be far from ruined if it has to be kept for an extra couple of hours.

Italian style chicken breasts

½-1 chicken breast per person, depending on size
½ tsp dried marjoram or mixed herbs
1 tin chopped tomatoes with onions
1 tsp Worcestershire Sauce
A few olives (optional)

Rinse chicken breasts and pat dry. Place in slow cooker. Combine remaining ingredients and pour over chicken breasts. Cover and cook on Low for 5-7 hours. Serve with noodles or brown rice and a green salad.

Coq au vin

This classical dish is ideal for, say, an after theatre party, and there is plenty of room in a 3 litre Slow Cooker to double up on the quantities - either for entertaining purposes or for freezer portions:

For four people, use:

4 chicken joints, skinned	1-2 tbsp flour
15ml (1tbsp) olive oil	100g (4oz) streaky bacon, chopped
1 large onion, chopped	300ml (½pint) chicken stock
300-600ml (½-1 pint) red wine	100g (4oz) button mushrooms, sliced
1 bay leaf	2 cloves
1 bouquet garni	Sea salt and freshly ground black pepper

Heat the oil in a frying pan. Coat the chicken joints in seasoned flour and fry on all sides. Transfer to the Slow Cooker. Add the bacon and onion to the pan and soften, but do not brown. Add the remaining flour and all other ingredients. Bring to the boil, stirring continuously and pour over the chicken joints. Cook on High for 3 ½-5 hours (4 ½-8 hours on Slow/Auto).

PUDDINGS

Most of us who lead busy lives simply don't have time for puddings, but the Slow Cooker can be useful for week-end treat puddings - or again for entertaining.

Winter fruit salad

Use equal quantities (approximately 100g/4oz) of dried prunes, apricots, apples, pears and raisins. Place in Slow Cooker with juice of half a lemon and 600ml (1 pint) water and soak overnight. Next day, cook on High 3-4 hours or Auto/Slow for 4-5 hours. Serve hot or cold with plain, live yoghurt, for breakfast or as a pudding.

Baked apples

If you have a glut of apples in the autumn, it is a good idea to bake up to six at a time ready to be eaten hot or cold (they can also be frozen individually or in a freezer box if you reach the stage where you never want to see another apple!).

Grease the cooking pot with a little butter. Run a sharp knife around the centre of each apple to score the skin and prevent it bursting open. Fill with a mixture of raisins, chopped dried apricots or prunes, almonds, hazelnuts and/or walnuts. This should be sufficiently sweet, but if you need a little extra, add a little fructose or raw cane sugar. Pour ¼- ½ pint boiling water around the apples and cook on High for 2-3 hours (Auto 4-7 hours) depending on the variety of apple.

Pears in red wine

Another excellent way of using up the autumn glut, and a good party dish. For four large, or six medium pears, use

50g (2 oz) raw cane sugar

400ml (¾pint) red wine

Juice and rind of half a lemon (scrubbed!)

2 cloves

Switch on the Slow Cooker. Add the sugar, wine, lemon rind, juice and cloves. Stir until the sugar dissolves. Peel the pears leaving them whole and complete with stalks. Place them in the Slow Cooker with the stalks standing upwards. Baste with the syrup. Cook on High for 3-5 hours (Slow/Auto 4-9 hours). Turn the pears from time to time if possible to ensure even colour. Serve with plain, live yoghurt or crème fraiche.

Rice pudding

125g (4oz) brown pudding rice
24fl oz (750mls) milk or soya milk
1 heaped tbs raw cane sugar
Nutmeg (preferably freshly grated)

Wash the rice well and place in Slow Cooker with the remaining ingredients. Cover and cook on High for 2½ - 3 hours (Slow/Auto 3-5 hours). If possible, stir during the last hour of cooking.

Christmas pudding

I'm a bit lazy about making Christmas pudding these days, and there are some really delicious ones to be bought now, including wheat-free ones. To heat your pudding, pour 8 fl oz/250mls hot water into the slow cooker. Add the bowl with the covered pudding, cover the slow cooker and cook on Low for 12-14 hours. Try serving with crème fraiche.

Bread and butter pudding

4 thin slices wholemeal or wheat-free bread, buttered
4 oz/125g dried mixed fruit
1-2 tbsp raw cane sugar
2 free range eggs
1 pint milk, soya, rice or oat milk
1 tsp vanilla

Halve the bread slices and arrange in layers, buttered side up, in a greased ovenproof dish which will fit inside the slow cooker. Sprinkle each layer with the fruit and a little sugar. Lightly beat the eggs, milk and vanilla until mixed and strain over the bread. Allow to stand for 10-60 minutes. Cover the bowl with foil or a lid. Put 8 fl oz/250mls hot water in the slow cooker, place the bowl of pudding, cover and cook on High for 3-4 hours.

Under Pressure

Pressure cooking - methods and recipes

I had always been somewhat nervous of the old-fashioned pressure cookers, but after spending a little time with Tefal UK Ltd, the manufacturers of a new breed of pressure cooker, I no longer have that feeling that it is going to explode any minute. Contemporary pressure cookers or "X-press Cookers" as they are sometimes called, usually have a heavy plate welded to the bottom, which helps prevent burning and evenly distributes the heat. Several safety features are built in so that it is virtually impossible for the cooker to explode, thereby ensuring that your meal remains in the pan rather than having to be scraped off the ceiling.

Advantages of pressure cooking

Preservation of nutrients. Because of reduced cooking time, fewer nutrients are lost during the cooking process. Also, because the container is sealed, less nutrients are lost due to evaporation.

Energy efficiency. Once the required pressure is reached, the cooking temperature increases and cooking time decreases; sometimes by as much as one third or even a half.

Cost efficiency. Pressure cooking has a tenderizing effect on protein fibres, thus enabling a cheaper cut of meat to be used.

Versatility. To-day's pressure cookers come with trivets and steamer baskets to enable several different cooking options and easy removal of food. They are available in a variety of sizes, but a large (10 quart) size is a good buy so that you can cook larger quantities of soups, casseroles etc. and freeze leftover portions for a future meal/s. They are also ideal for making different types of stock. Also, although you can cook small quantities in a large pressure cooker, the converse is not true.

Safety. Modern pressure cookers have multiple built-in safety features. The combination of a steam release valve, a manual pressure release valve and a lid gasket virtually eliminates the possibility of an explosion. Also, pressure will only build up if the lid is properly sealed, and the lid can only be removed when no pressure remains. However, **it is essential to read the manufacturers instructions** before using your pressure cooker, and not to exceed the fill line (this is usually about two-thirds full).

Adapting your own recipes.

> As a general rule, cut the cooking time down from a third to half the cooking time in your original recipe..
>
> Allow approximately 4 fl oz of liquid for each 10 minutes of cooking time. For steaming vegetables, allow approx. 8 fl oz liquid for each 10 minutes of cooking
>
> Season dishes very lightly at first, since pressure cooking retains more of the food's flavour and nutrients. After releasing the pressure, taste the food and, if necessary adjust the seasonings.

SOUPS

If you add pulses (beans, lentils etc.) to your soup, they do tend to foam and could possibly cause the pressure cooker to clog. Adding 1 tbs. olive oil per cup of dried beans will prevent this.

If necessary, reduce the liquid content of your original recipe so that it doesn't exceed the maximum fill line of your pressure cooker. You can always add in more liquid once it is cooked.

Because vegetables cook so quickly in a pressure cooker, you may prefer to add them towards the end of the cooking time.

Due to the large amount of liquid in soups, the cooker will take about 20 minutes to reach pressure.

CHICKEN, MEAT OR FISH STOCK

Although the making of stock does not strictly come into the sphere of not having time to cook, personally, I think this tastes so much better than stock cubes and is so easy to make in a pressure cooker.

Place any bones or left-over pieces of meat in the cooker with cold water and bring to the boil. Remove any scum that rises to the top of the cooker. When scum has stopped forming, you may add a chopped onion and carrot, and perhaps some herbs, season lightly, bring to high pressure, reduce the heat and cook for 30 minutes. After releasing pressure, strain and check seasoning. Pieces of meat may be added to soup. Put the stock into the fridge and remove any solidified fat.

MEATS AND POULTRY

When adapting recipes for braised meats, allow 20 minutes of cooking time per pound of meat. Use 8 fl oz liquid for the first pound and 4 fl oz for each additional pound.

When in doubt about the proper cooking time for meats or poultry, undercook the food rather than take a chance of over-cooking it. It can always be re-sealed and cooked for a few more minutes.

For steam roasting poultry, brown it first in olive oil. Add the trivet and 8 fl oz water to the pressure cooker. Cook for 5 minutes per pound of unstuffed poultry and 8 minutes per pound for stuffed poultry (weighed before stuffing).

Remove the skin from the chicken before the chicken before pressure cooking to reduce fat content.

RICE AND BEANS

For plain, brown, rice, bring the water to boil and add rice. Cook under high pressure for about 8 minutes. If you use white rice, cooking time takes about 6-7 minutes but is, of course, almost totally devoid of nutrients.

For rice pilaf, heat a little olive oil in the cooker and sauté the rice for 2-3 minutes. Add liquid and bring to a boil; proceed as for plain rice.

Dried beans will double in volume when soaked. Take care to soak them in a container that is large enough to accommodate the quantity.

It is not strictly necessary to pre-soak beans for pressure cooking, but soaking does reduce the gas-producing qualities of beans as they are water-soluble. Always drain the soaking water from the beans and cook with fresh water. Soaking also cuts down the cooking time and keeps the bean skins from separating from the flesh.

Hot Soaking Method - Use 2 pints water and 1 tsp salt for every 8 oz dried beans. Place the ingredients in the pressure cooker and bring up to low pressure. Remove the cooker from the heat, release the pressure and allow to stand for 4 hours. Drain and discard the soaking water.

When adapting bean recipes, use 24 fl oz/770 ml fresh water for every 8 oz/225g. beans for cooking. Do not add salt at this stage or the beans will remain tough. Adding 1 tbs. olive oil will prevent the beans from clogging the pressure cooker's vents. Bring the cooker up to high pressure and cook as follows:

Bean Type	pre-soaked	unsoaked
	(minutes after reaching full pressure)	
Aduki	6-8	15-20
Black-eyed		9-11
Chick peas	10-12	28-30

Bean Type	pre-soaked	unsoaked
	(minutes after reaching full pressure)	
Kidney	9-12	20-25
Lentils (brown or green)		20-25
Lentils (red)		3-4
Lima	4-7	12-15
Peas (split)	10-12	28-30
Pinto	4-7	22-25
Soybeans	10-12	28-35

This is an excellent way of providing a nourishing meal at very low cost. On the other hand, you could use tinned, ready-cooked beans, chick peas and lentils.

VEGETABLES

Use the steamer basket whenever possible to keep vegetables out of the cooking water. This way the vitamins do not leach into the water.

To avoid overcooking, use the minimum amount of water indicated in the manufacturer's instructions and bring to a boil before sealing the cooker. Distribute the vegetables evenly in the steamer basket to ensure even cooking.

Vegetables cook very quickly in a pressure cooker, so watch the time carefully. When adapting recipes, keep the cooking time to a minimum; usually about one third of the time for conventional cooking.

When cooking more than one vegetable, cut the shorter-cooking vegetables in larger pieces than the longer-cooking ones.

Hopefully, the following selection of recipes will either get you going on pressure cooking, or inspire you to get your old one out of storage.

Tuscan tomato and basil soup

60ml/2fl oz olive oil
1 onion, coarsely chopped
1 x 13 oz tin tomatoes
10 basil leaves
50g (2 oz) Parmesan cheese, grated

300 ml (½ pint) stock
2 cloves garlic
1 bay leaf
1 sprig thyme
seasoning to taste

Heat the oil in the cooker, add the onion, thyme , bay leaf and garlic. Cook for 3 minutes over a medium heat. Add the tomatoes and stock. Bring to pressure over a high heat, then reduce heat and cook for 3 minutes. Release pressure, remove lid and stir. Add ripped basil, Parmesan and seasoning to taste.

Creamy leek and potato soup

2 large leeks (white part only)
½ medium onion, coarsely chopped
pinch nutmeg and cayenne
½ pint stock
4 oz fresh salmon cut into thin slices

25g (l oz) unsalted butter
2 medium potatoes, thinly sliced
150ml (½ pint) milk or soya milk
2 tbs. chopped dill
1 tbs. snipped chives

Heat the butter in the cooker, fry the leeks, onion, potatoes, nutmeg and cayenne for 3 minutes over a medium heat. Add the stock and milk. Lock the lid in place and over a high heat bring to pressure level 1. Reduce heat and cook for five minutes. Release the pressure and remove lid. Pour contents of the pan into a liquidizer and blend until smooth. Return to cooker and add dill and salmon. Cook over medium heat for 3 minutes with lid off. Season to taste and serve. Garnish with snipped chives.

Fish and corn chowder

25g/1oz unsalted butter
1 onion, finely chopped
2 carrots, finely chopped
1 clove garlic, crushed
½ pint fish stock
250g/8 oz tinned corn kernels, drained

50g/2oz streaky bacon cut into strips
2 stalks celery, finely sliced
12 tsp thyme leaves
375g/12 oz white fish, cubed
¾ pint milk or soya milk
2 tbsp chopped parsley   seasoning to taste

Heat butter in the cooker, add the bacon and cook over a medium heat, stirring until the bacon begins to release some of its fat (about 3 minutes). Add the onion, celery, carrot, thyme and garlic, and cook for 3 minutes. Add the fish chunks, stock and bay leaf. Lock lid in place and over a high heat, bring to pressure level 1. Reduce heat and cook for 4 minutes. Release pressure, remove lid and bay leaf. Add remaining ingredients and heat through. Season to taste.

Cream of asparagus soup

25g/1 oz butter
2 onions, chopped
1 kg/2lb fresh asparagus (reserve tips for garnish)
450ml/16fl oz milk or soya milk

25g/1 oz olive oil
4 medium potatoes, diced
900ml/30 fl oz chicken stock
½ tsp. nutmeg

Heat butter and oil in the pressure cooker over medium heat and sauté onions until softened. Stir in potatoes and asparagus and add chicken stock. Season lightly and bring to a boil. Seal the cooker, bring up to pressure, reduce heat to stabilize pressure and cook for 7 minutes.

Remove cooker from heat and release pressure. Cool slightly and liquidize. Return to pressure cooker and add milk, nutmeg and asparagus tips. Reheat gently until tips are cooked (do NOT boil).

Lemon curried pea soup

1 large onion, sliced
2 stalks celery, sliced
2 tsp curry powder
500g/1 lb fresh or frozen peas
16 fl oz/¾ pint milk or soya milk
1 tsp grated lemon peel

2 carrots, sliced
2 medium potatoes, sliced
2 cloves garlic
30 fl oz (1 ½ pints) chicken stock
1 tbs. lemon juice
Seasoning to taste

Add onion, carrots, celery, potatoes, garlic, lemon juice, lemon peel, curry powder, 15 fl oz/¾ pint of the chicken stock and peas to the pressure cooker and bring to the boil. Seal cooker, bring up to high pressure, reduce the heat to stabilize pressure and cook for 5 minutes.

Remove cooker from heat and release pressure. Purée hot soup with a food processor or blender until smooth and return to cooker. Add remaining chicken stock and milk or soya milk. Heat gently uncovered over low heat until just heated through. Taste and adjust seasonings.

Tri-colour pepper spread

1 red pepper
1 green pepper
1 yellow pepper
olive oil

100ml/4 fl oz water
1 tbsp anchovy paste
125g/4 oz chopped olives
French bread or crispbreads

Cut peppers into matchstick strips. Place in the steamer basket in the pressure cooker and add water. Seal cooker; bring up to high pressure, reduce heat to stabilize pressure and cook for 3 minutes.

Remove from heat and release pressure. Remove steamer basket and pour out excess water; wipe cooker dry. Coat bottom with olive oil and sauté steamed pepper mixture until browned. Add olives and anchovy paste. Check seasoning.

Meatball soup

A delicious Mexican soup which makes a meal on its own simply serve with a crisp tossed salad and crispy bread or tortillas.

2 tbs. olive oil
2 cloves garlic, crushed
1 egg, beaten
60fl oz/3pints stock
750g/1 ½ lb minced lamb

1 onion, chopped
80g/3 oz long-grain rice
8 oz/225g jar tomato sauce
1 tbsp chopped fresh mint leaves
2 carrots, diced

Heat oil in the pressure cooker over medium heat and sauté onion and garlic until softened. Add tomato sauce, stock and carrots and bring to boil. In a separate bowl, mix together lamb, rice, egg, mint and a little seasoning. Form mixture into 2 ½ cm/1-inch balls. Drop meatballs into boiling stock mixture. Seal cooker, bring up to high pressure, reduce heat to stabilize pressure and cook for 10 minutes. A small packet of frozen peas may be added, in which case simmer for 1-2 minutes.

Prosciutto-wrapped leeks

900g/2lbs large leeks
100g/4 fl oz water
125g/4 oz prosciutto, thinly sliced

2 tbsp olive oil
50g/2 oz Parmigiano Reggiano

Trim leeks and cut in half lengthwise, leaving the root end intact. Wash thoroughly and lay in steamer basket. Add water. Seal cooker, bring up to high pressure, reduce heat to stabilize pressure and cook for about 2 minutes.
Remove from heat and release pressure. Wrap each leek section with a slice of prosciutto, place in a baking dish, drizzle with olive oil and sprinkle with Parmesan.

Braised orange fennel

4 bulbs fennel
100ml/4 fl oz water
2 tbsp olive oil
seasoning to taste

1 clove garlic, crushed
100ml/4 fl oz orange juice
1 tsp brown sugar

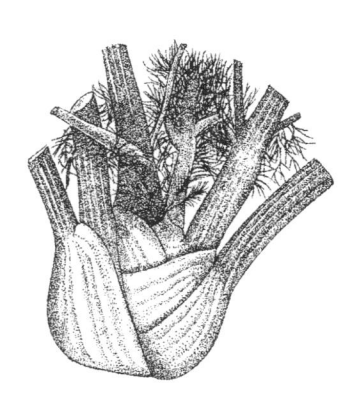

Cut fennel bulbs in half and place in the steamer basket with water. Seal cooker, bring up to high pressure, reduce heat to stabilize pressure and cook 3-5 minutes depending on size of bulbs. Remove cooker from heat and release pressure. Remove fennel, pour out remaining water and wipe dry. Put oil into cooker over medium heat and add sugar, stirring to dissolve. Add garlic and partially cooked fennel. Cook until browned on one side, then turn bulbs and add orange juice and light seasoning. Remove heat when second side is browned.

Chickpea and spinach curry

50g/2 oz butter or olive oil
½ red pepper, diced
2 tbsp pine nuts
300g/10oz dried chick peas (soaked overnight)
450ml/ ¾ pint vegetable stock
4 handfuls spinach

1 onion, finely chopped
6 dried apricots, diced
2 cloves garlic, finely chopped
2 tsp curry powder
2 tomatoes, chopped

Gently heat butter or oil in the cooker. Add all ingredients except tomato and spinach. Bring to pressure, reduce heat and cook for 15 minutes on pressure level 1. Release pressure, remove lid and fold in tomatoes and spinach. Cook for 3 minutes, season to taste.

Quinoa seafood salad

350g/12 oz quinoa

50ml/2 fl oz balsamic vinegar

900ml/1 ½ pints water

2½ tbs soy sauce

4 spring onions, chopped

2 ½ tbs grated ginger

125-175g/4-6 oz sugar-snap peas

½ cucumber, sliced

3 tbs sesame oil

350g/¾ lb prawns

2 tsp honey

fresh coriander

¼ tsp cayenne pepper

Toast quinoa in the pressure cooker over a medium heat, stirring until lightly browned. Add water, seal cooker, bring up to high pressure, reduce heat to stabilize pressure and cook for 4 minutes.

Remove cooker from heat and release pressure. Allow to stand for 5 minutes, then transfer to a bowl to cool. Add peas, onions, cucumber, prawns and coriander. In a screwtop jar, put vinegar, soy sauce, ginger, sesame oil, honey and cayenne and shake until well blended. Pour over salad and toss well.

Pot roast chicken with puy lentils

25g (1 oz) olive oil
300ml (½ pint chicken stock)
1 carrot, peeled and diced
1 tsp soft thyme leaves
1 glass red wine

1 free-range chicken
2 slices smoked streaky bacon, diced
1 stick celery, diced
2 bay leaves
125g (4 oz) lentils

Brown the chicken in olive oil until golden. Remove and re-place on the trivet in the cooker. Pour on the stock. Lock lid in place, bring to pressure, reduce heat to medium and cook for 5 minutes on pressure level 1. Place the bacon in a separate pan with a little olive oil and cook until starting to brown. Add onion, garlic, celery, carrot, thyme and bay leaf. Cook for 3 minutes, then add red wine and lentils. Release pressure and remove lid from the cooker. Spoon the bacon and lentil mixture down the side of the chicken. Lock lid in position and bring to pressure. Cook for a further 8 minutes on pressure level 2. Garnish with parsley if available.

Italian stuffed peppers

2 red peppers
2 green peppers
25g/1oz pine nuts
300ml/½ pt Passata tomatoes
50g/2oz onions, finely chopped

50g/2oz wholemeal breadcrumbs (or rice)
100g/4oz cheddar cheese
Seasoning
1 tsp dried mixed herbs
1 tbsp olive oil

Heat oil in the cooker, add onion and cook until soft. Add the breadcrumbs or rice, cheese, Passata, herbs, pine nuts and seasoning. Stir until combined. Slice off the pepper tops and remove the seeds. Divide the tomato mixture between the peppers. Replace lids and sit in the steaming basket. Rinse out pressure cooker, place the trivet in the base, lowering the steaming basket on top. Pour 400ml/¾ pint water into the base. Lock lid in place and over a high heat bring to pressure level 1. Reduce heat and cook for 7 minutes. Reduce steam quickly.

Cannellini bean and goat cheese salad

250g/8oz dried cannellini beans (soaked overnight)
2 tbsp extra virgin olive oil
1 tbsp freshly squeezed lemon juice
4 tbsp fresh coriander leaves, chopped
3 tbsp parsley, chopped
1 chilli (optional), finely chopped
250g/8oz goats' cheese cut in 1 cm (½") cubes
sea salt and black pepper to taste

Drain the beans and rinse. Place in the cooker with 600ml/2 pint water and 1 tbsp olive oil. Lock lid in place and bring to pressure. Reduce heat and cook for 20 minutes at level 1. Release pressure, remove lid and drain beans. In a medium size bowl, combine the warm beans and all the remaining ingredients. Check seasoning and serve with a green salad and sun-dried tomato bread.

Spiced red wine pears

4 Conference pears, peeled but not cored
A little soft brown sugar (to taste)
3"/7cm cinnamon stick
¼ tsp grated nutmeg
2 bay leaves
rind of 1 orange and 1 lemon
8 juniper berries
3 cloves
3 cardamom pods, crushed
300ml/½ pint red wine

Cut flat bases for each of the pears and stand them upright in the bottom of the cooker. Add the remaining ingredients. Lock the lid in position and bring to pressure level 1. Reduce heat and cook for 5-10 minutes depending on the ripeness of the pears. Release pressure, remove lid and lift the pears out of the cooker and place in a bowl. Check liquid for sweetness and boil until it is reduced by half. Pour over the pears and refrigerate overnight, turning them until they turn red. Serve with yogurt or crème fraiche.

12 Feeding The Family

If eating healthily is important for adults, it is even *more* so for children. There is mounting evidence that the basis of good health in adult years is laid down both during pregnancy and in the child's formative years. Incidence of hyperactivity and Attention Deficit Disorder (ADD) has a nutritional connection. Teenage girls with Supermodel aspirations are showing early signs of osteoporosis and hormone imbalances. At the other end of the scale, obesity in children is becoming increasingly common, leading to an 80% likelihood of obesity in adulthood. Young boys are plagued with acne due to diets which are high in fats and sugars, and low in zinc and Vitamin A. A national survey showed that approximately one third of the UK adult population; 44% of teenagers; and 50% of children (1½ to 4½ years) do not receive the recommended nutrient intake for Vitamin A.

Reference Nutrient Intakes (RNIs) for women aged 19-50 years (UK)									
NUTRIENT	UNITS	RNI		%<RNI		LRNI		%<LRNI	
		Men	Women	Men	Women	Men	Women	Men	Women
Vitamin A	mcg	700	600	27	31	300	250	2	3
Thiamin	mg	*	*	-	-	*	*	-	-
Riboflavin	mg	1.3	1.1	12	21	0.8	0.8	1	8
Niacin	mg	17	13	1	2	11	9	-	-
Vitamin B6	mg	1.4	1.2	6	22	1.0	0.8	-	-
Vitamin B12	mcg	1.5	1.5	1	4	1.0	1.0	0	1
Folate	mcg	200	200	12	47	100	100	0	4
Vitamin C	mg	40	40	26	34	10	10	0	1
Calcium	mg	700	700	25	48	400	400	2	10
Magnesium	mg	300	270	42	72	190	150	8	13
Potassium	mg	3500	3500	65	94	2000	2000	6	27
iron	mg	8.7	14.8	12	89	4.7	8	1	26
Zinc	mg	9.5	7	31	31	5.5	4	2	4
Copper	mg	1.2	1.2	24	59	(a)	(a)	-	-
Iodine	mcg	140	140	9	32	70	70	1	3
Selenium	mcg	75	60	-	-	40	40	-	-

* dependent on calorie intake (RNI, men 1mg/2550kcal; women 0.8mg/1940kcal); -, unknown at present ; (a), no set LRNI at present

Although a good quality supplement of vitamins, minerals and essential fatty acids is undoubtedly helpful, it should be thought of as an adjunct to a healthy diet only. Nutrients provided by daily food should *always* come first.

No one has ever suggested that this is an easy task! We simply cannot understand why one or two members of the family are faddy and difficult eaters, while the others have a healthy appetite, all having been brought up on the same diet. I certainly find that an increasing number of children have allergies to the dairy products which they consume in great quantities, leaving them little inclination to eat other foods.

Increasingly, families no longer eat together at the table, with children helping themselves to easy-to-cook foods with little or no nutrients.

Children need high quality proteins, as many fruit and vegetables as they can be persuaded to eat; and adequate carbohydrates in their complex (whole) form. The more refined the carbohydrates, the less the nutrient content *and* the more nutrients are required to process such foods. High fat foods prevent the up-take of essential fatty acids which are needed for brain cells, good skin and healthy hormones to name but a few. Digestion of the foods is also extremely important if the benefits of good food are to be felt. And without going so far as to suggest that each mouthful be chewed "x" number of times, it really is important to see that meals are well masticated and eaten, sitting down, in a relaxed atmosphere.

Some children decide independently to become vegetarian and if they are the first in the family to do so, it is only too easy just to add, for example, cheese to every meal. For children with a tendency to produce a lot of catarrh, this can lead to increasing problems with ear infections, colds, tonsillitis etc. New research also shows that cow's milk protein may be a major contributory factor triggering the onset of childhood, insulin-dependent diabetes in genetically susceptible children. Cheese is also high in saturated fats, with their ensuing problems. This naturally leads to the question "but how will we get enough calcium?". Calcium from milk is not, in fact, utilized very efficiently by the human body. It is low in magnesium, which is a mineral needed to ensure the uptake and utilization of calcium. Sources of calcium which are more efficiently used by the body are: broccoli, sesame seeds including tahini, almonds, molasses ……etc, not forgetting soya products - see Chapter 6 "Treat yourself to Tofu".

Learning to cope with the new vegetarian is not easy, but it is so important that the growing child is provided with sufficient quantity and quality of proteins. In the case of "mixed households" - vegetarian and carnivorous - why not alternate the type of cooking, taking it in turns for one type to have a freshly cooked meal, and the other one which has been frozen from the last time you cooked it? When a child suddenly decides, quite independently, that he no longer wishes to eat meat, it is all too easy to substitute cheese or simply to serve up the remaining part of the meal. Although initially requiring a little time and patience, it is well worth getting children to take an interest in preparing their own food, experimenting with recipes and researching food values and healthy diets. Persuading the rest of the family that vegetarian food is not just "cheese and lettuce" is a useful way of increasing the variety of food that they might eat.

On the other side of the coin, however, there are children in vegetarian families who would definitely do better with a little meat, chicken and fish in their diet.

Where there are babies in the family, most meals can be liquidized successfully, and then mashed or cut into tiny pieces as they become able to cope with family meals

How to cope with the faddy eater

The most important thing is to set an example by, whenever possible, all sitting down together to a nourishing meal. Even quite young children understand the concept of healthy food when you explain the beneficial effect it has on them, just as they can often see the opposite effect when they eat a food which is high in, for example, sugar, fat and colourings. Sometimes a compromise can be reached without too much trouble - a tofu burger, a beefburger made from organically reared beef, or a fish finger (recipe below).

Sometimes children come under pressure from friends at school to eat the latest, heavily advertised fad food, and are ridiculed for arriving at the lunch table with a box of unfamiliar-looking wholesome food. Just make it as appetizing and tasty as possible in the hope that your child's food will catch on as an alternative.

A note on sugar, salt, msg (monosodium glutamate) and fats

Highly processed foods such as burgers and pizza are usually high in such additives and there is no doubt about it - they are highly addictive!   You may therefore find that, in order to make a radical change towards healthy eating, it needs to be done gradually. As far as sugar is concerned, you could try using fructose (not too much, it is **very** sweet), rice or barley syrup, or a substance known as fructo-oligosaccharides - commonly known as FOS. This is an indigestible sugar which provides a good source of fibre and a banquet for the beneficial bacteria which live in the colon. Introduce it gradually, though, as it has similar effects to eating Jerusalem artichokes! They both contain the beneficial, but wind-forming compound inulin. A commonly asked question is "what about artificial sweeteners?" to which the short answer is "Don't". All artificial sweeteners have a down-side. Saccharine has been found to cause cancer in laboratory animals; aspartame is broken down in the body to form methanol and formaldehyde, both of which cause health problems, and I have seen children who become severely hyperactive when consuming foods and drinks which contain aspartame. In fact, it accounts for about 75% of the adverse food reactions which actually get reported to the US Food and Drug Administration.

In the short-term, salt can be exchanged for one of the excellent low-sodium substitutes. Most of these contain potassium, which tends to be low in the average diet and is essential for healthy nerves and muscles; blood sugar control and fluid balance in the body. In the long-term, however, it is best to persuade the tastebuds that good food does not need to be salty food. If you enjoy strong flavours, try increasing garlic, herbs, olives, anchovies, soya sauce, seaweed and umiboshi plums.

Monosodium glutamate (msg) is the flavour enhancer found in Chinese cooking and so many processed and manufactured foods. Again, it is fairly addictive as it can change the rather nondescript taste of such foods into something with a strong and distinctive flavour. Try asking your local Chinese restaurant for a meal without this additive and you will immediately see the difference! Healthy alternatives include miso - there are many varieties with strengths varying from mild to quite strong - soya sauce, shoyu and tamari.

Above all, make family mealtimes happy occasions and try to stay relaxed when one of the children turns up his nose at your delicious (to you) and healthy offering. We all lose our appetite from time to time and this may be the reason. No child is going to starve himself to death, so please resist the temptation to give biscuits, crisps and sweets in between, or instead of, meals. Some children will latch on to one particular food and demand it at every meal. As long as it contains a balance of nutrients, they will come to no harm and will eventually become bored and want to move on to something different. Try to set a good example by ensuring that *your food* is varied and appetizing.

Although it takes the patience of a saint, do encourage children to "help" in the kitchen whenever possible - perhaps just chopping vegetables which they enjoy nibbling on raw - and even if you loathe cooking, try not to show it. Children love "baking" buns and biscuits - just make sure they use healthy ingredients. Provide them with food cutters to cut vegetables into fancy "animal" shapes, for example.

Piperade

1 green or red pepper
2 large tomatoes
A little olive oil and a small knob of butter

medium onion
4 free range eggs
a generous pinch of herbs

Heat the oil and butter. Chop the onions and peppers and fry gently for about 5 minutes. Add the tomatoes, chopped (de-seeded if you have the time). Beat the eggs, season with sea salt and freshly ground pepper and herbs. Add to the vegetables and stir well until lightly cooked. Serve with crusty bread and a crisp salad.

Smoked salmon with potatoes

1 lb/450g potatoes

juice of 1-2 lemons

Sea salt and freshly ground black pepper

8 oz/225g smoked salmon pieces

2 tbsp Extra Virgin olive oil

A few snippings of chives

Boil the potatoes and turn them into a serving dish. Add the salmon pieces and sprinkle over the olive oil, juice of 1 lemon and seasoning. Add extra oil or lemon juice if needed. Decorate with chives and serve with a large green salad.

White fish (haddock, cod, coley etc) on lentils.

Bake or steam one portion of fish per person. Drain and rinse the contents of a 14oz/400g can of brown lentils. Heat gently and put onto a serving dish. Lay the fish portions on the lentils and decorate with slices of tomato.

Mediterranean mackerel

1 mackerel fillet per person (ask your fishmonger to do this for you)

Olive oil an oven-proof dish; place fillets, brush with more olive oil + herbs. Cook for approximately 20 minutes in a moderate oven, 350ºF/180ºC/Gas Mark 4

Pasta served with hemp pesto
see chapter 5 Going Nuts; Running to seed

Pasta with various sauces

Jacket potatoes *(see Dressing for Dinner chapter 17)*

Use sweet potatoes as an alternative sometimes. For real speed, put the potatoes in the Slow Cooker in the morning. The following can be added in a couple of minutes to make a nourishing meal:

Yoghurt with chives or herbs
Sardines in tomato sauce, or olive oil with a squeeze of lemon
Prawns or tuna in a lemon juice vinaigrette or yoghurt dressing
Tofu Dressing (see Treat Yourself to Tofu - Chapter 6)
Sautéed mushrooms

Bolognese

1 lb/450g minced beef, turkey, quorn or TVP
1 onion
1-2 cloves garlic
1 tin tomatoes
1 tbsp olive oil
Mixed herbs as available
2 tbsp tomato purée

Gently heat the oil. Add the onion, chopped, and garlic and fry the onion until transparent. Add the meat or vegetarian option and brown, then add the tomato pure and tin of tomatoes. Chopped carrots and celery can also be added in. Simmer for approximately 20 minutes, or longer if time permits. (This is an excellent recipe for the Slow Cooker). Serve with pasta and scatter grated Parmesan cheese and herbs on top.

Lentil bolognese

175g/6oz tin brown lentils	1 x 400g/14 oz tin tomatoes
1 medium onion, finely chopped	2 tbsp tomato puree
15ml/1tbsp olive oil	Tamari or soy sauce
2 cloves garlic, crushed	350g/12 oz mushrooms, sliced
1 tsp dried herbs	Freshly ground black pepper

Heat the oil in a large pan and fry the onion and garlic until transparent. Add the mushrooms, lentils and herbs and cook for 10 minutes. Stir in the tomatoes and purée. Cover and cook for 20-25 minutes. Season with tamari or soy sauce and pepper.

Celery and almond sauce

2 tbsp olive oil	150ml/¼ pint vegetable stock
225g/8 oz onions, finely chopped	2 cloves garlic, crushed
225g/8oz celery, finely chopped	100g/4oz slivered almonds.

Heat the oil and gently fry the onions and celery with the garlic for 2-3 minutes. Cover and continue cooking for 10 mins or until the vegetables are really tender. Add the stock, cover and cook for another 10 minutes until the sauce is creamy. Season to taste. Lightly brown the almonds in the oven or under the grill. Serve sauce over freshly cooked pasta with almonds sprinkled over.

Broccoli and anchovy

1 tin anchovies in olive oil
1 onion, finely chopped.
225g/8 oz broccoli
A little stock

Drain the oil from the tin of anchovies into a medium-sized pan. Heat gently and fry the onion until transparent. Add the broccoli cut into bite-sized pieces, cover and cook until al dente. You may need to add a little more olive oil and some stock to moisten.

Hummus

1 x 400g/14oz tin of chick peas
1-2 cloves garlic, crushed
2-3 tbsp tahini
1-2 tbsp olive oil
Juice of half a lemon
1 tbsp olive oil
2-3 tbsp vegetable stock
Sea salt and freshly ground black pepper

Drain the chick peas and put into a blender with the lemon juice, garlic and oil. Blend well, adding a little stock if it becomes too thick. Add the tahini and blend until creamy. You may wish to add more lemon juice.

Serve with salad and wholemeal toast or oatcakes.

Bean salad

Open a tin of haricot, kidney, aduki or black-eyed beans. Drain and rinse. Add 2 chopped tomatoes, a red pepper and 2 tbsp French dressing. Season to taste and serve with rice or baked or new potatoes.

Fishfingers

Cut a piece of your favourite fresh fish into 2 x ½ " pieces. Roll the fish in fine oatmeal or ground almonds with a little seasoning. Gently fry in olive oil for 1-2 minutes per side. Serve with fresh lemon wedges.

Salmon fingers

Allowing one salmon steak per person, cut each steak into "fingers" and coat with oatmeal and chopped parsley. Gently fry in olive oil for 2 minutes per side. Serve with mashed potato and broccoli.

Bean and tuna salad

1 tin of tuna in olive oil
1 tin of butter or flageolet beans.

Flake tuna, retaining olive oil. Add beans and sufficient fresh lemon juice to make a dressing. Add seasoning and herbs to taste, and a little chopped red or spring onion.

Have with brown rice, Ryvita, oat or ricecakes.

Roasted vegetables

Put 1-2 tbsp olive oil into a baking tin. Cut sweet potatoes in half lengthways; quarter red, yellow and/or green peppers; halve red onion. Turn all vegetables to give a light coating of oil and cook at 190C/375F Gas Mark 5. After ¼ hour, add quartered tomatoes. Serve with grilled chops, fish, veggie burgers or a little grated cheese.

Frittata (a family-sized omelette)

Allow two free-range eggs per person.
1 large leek
1 red pepper
(or any combination of vegetables such as red or spring onions, cooked potato, mushrooms, green pepper, celery etc).

Heat the frying pan over a moderate heat and add 1-2 tbsp olive oil. When hot, put in your chosen vegetables, finely chopped, and fry gently until soft. Add the eggs, well beaten, and a handful of fresh herbs (or 1 tsp dried if not available) and pour over the vegetables. 1oz/25g of grated, strongly flavoured cheese may also be added.

Reduce heat as much as possible and cook until the sides are firm (this may take 10 minutes) then remove from the heat and put under the grill until the top is cooked (5-10 minutes). Divide into portions and serve immediately with a large green salad.

Chicken with rice and peas

300g/12oz Basmati rice
100g/4 oz frozen peas
1.6 litres/3 pints vegetable or chicken stock

1 large leek, finely sliced
100g/4oz frozen corn
1 chicken breast per person

Mix the rice, leeks, peas and corn together in a wide deep frying pan. Add the stock and stir well. Lay the chicken breasts on top of the rice, cover the pan, bring to the boil and simmer steadily until the rice has absorbed all the liquid and the chicken is cooked (approx. 30 minutes) Add more liquid if needed. Serve with a crunchy green vegetable or salad.

Braised salmon steaks

1 small leek, thinly sliced
1 tbsp olive oil
1 salmon steak per person
200g/7 oz chopped fresh spinach or thawed, frozen spinach
2 courgettes, sliced thickly
1 lemon

Gently fry the leek, courgettes and spinach in olive oil in a large frying pan for 4-5 minutes. Lay the salmon steaks on top and place a slice of lemon on each steak. Cover the pan and bring gently to simmer. Cook for 10-15 minutes or until the steaks are cooked through. Serve at once with the vegetables and a green salad.

Eggs florentine

For each serving use:

4 oz (100g) cooked, drained and chopped spinach (well-thawed frozen is fine)
1 tbs olive oil
1 egg
Sea salt, freshly ground black pepper and a little grated nutmeg
1 tbs Parmesan cheese

Heat the spinach in the olive oil and sprinkle with a couple of pinches of nutmeg. Place in an ovenproof dish and make a hollow for each egg. Carefully break eggs into hollows and sprinkle the cheese over it. Bake in a preheated oven at 350ºF/180ºC (Gas Mark 4) for about 15 minutes. Serve with wholemeal toast or baked potato.

Spicy sausage with lentils

4 Chorizos or good quality organic sausages or soya sausage (cooked)
1 green pepper (optional)
4 oz (200g) green lentils
1 onion
1 carrot
2 sticks celery (optional)
500ml/18fl oz water or stock
1 tbsp olive oil

Rinse the lentils and bring to the boil in water. Allow to simmer for approx. 30 minutes. Meanwhile, heat the olive oil and gently cook the vegetables until soft. Cut the sausage into small chunks; add to the vegetables. Then add all the ingredients to the lentils for the final five minutes of cooking.

Serve with a generous scattering of fresh parsley.

Prawn or squid provencal

1 lb/450g fresh, peeled prawns, or squid, ready cleaned and prepared if possible.
1 onion
1 green pepper
1 x 14oz/400g tin chopped tomatoes
2 oz/25g black olives (optional)
2 tbs olive oil
1 carrot
½ glass white wine (optional)
1-2 cloves garlic, crushed
Freshly ground black pepper

Heat the olive oil and add the chopped onion, prawns or pieces of squid and lightly cook before adding the chopped green pepper, carrot and black olives if using. Cook until soft, then add tomatoes and wine. Simmer gently for 40 minutes.

Serve with ciabatta bread and a large green salad.
For a vegan version of this recipe, substitute ½ inch cubes of tofu for the fish.

Basic risotto

1 onion
6 oz/150g whole grain (brown) rice
1 pint/600ml good vegetable or chicken stock
 2 tbsp olive oil
1-2 cloves garlic

Heat the olive oil in a large heavy-based pan and gently cook chopped onion and garlic. Fry until transparent. Add rice and lightly brown before adding the stock. Stir thoroughly and simmer gently 30-35 minutes.

Meanwhile, prepare the ingredients you wish to add here are a few ideas:

Left-over chicken cut into strips

Prawns

Chopped nuts (walnuts, almonds, hazelnuts)

Mushrooms, lightly sautéed

Chopped red or green peppers and/or celery

Flaked smoked haddock, gently poached but not for too long

Flaked left-over salmon

Smoked salmon pieces

Organic lamb's liver cut into small pieces and fried in olive oil

Marinated tofu

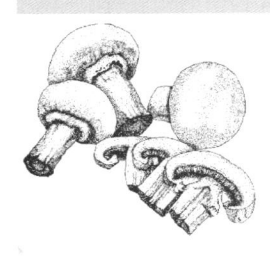

Vegetable "crisps"

Use a selection of organic vegetable peelings such as:
4 tbsp Olive oil (you may prefer to use a "light" version)

> Beetroot
> Carrot
> Sweet potato
> Parsnip
> Potatoes

Using a potato peeler, thickly peel chosen vegetables; pat dry on kitchen towel; heat until hot but not smoking; add vegetable peelings. Turn quickly until brown and crisp. Remove with a slotted spoon and place on kitchen paper to remove excess oil. Sprinkle with a little sea salt or gomasio. For those who like it, a light dusting of chilli powder will add a "bite". Serve straight away, although they can be reheated in the oven.

Spinach pie

1 lb/450g washed spinach
2 tbsp olive oil
1 small onion
1 tbsp wholemeal or alternative flour
Seasoning

3 free range eggs
4 fl oz /100ml water
2 cloves garlic
Parmesan cheese

Place eggs, oil, and water in blender, then add spinach, finely chopped onion, garlic and seasoning. Blend, adding more water if necessary. Pour into a bowl and add flour gradually, mixing in well, until mixture is creamy. Pour into a greased dish and grate parmesan on top. Bake for about 25 minutes at 350º F/180ºC/Gas Mark 4, until a light golden colour. Do not over-cook!

Tuna and anchovy pasta

2 tbsp olive oil
2 x 7oz/185g tins tuna fish
1 lemon
2 tbsp black olives (optional)

1 x 2oz/50g tin anchovies with their oil
1 medium leek, trimmed and very finely sliced
10oz/300g wholemeal, or alternative grain pasta
2 tbsp chopped parsley or coriander

Heat the oil in a pan. Chop the anchovies and add them, along with their oil and the leek and cook gently until the leeks are tender. Add the tuna and continue to cook very gently for another few minutes.

Meanwhile, cook the pasta according to the instructions on the pack. Add the olives, if used, lemon juice and the fresh herbs. Spoon over the pasta and serve with a green salad.

PUDDINGS

Quick fruit crumble

Fill an oven-proof dish with stewed fruit of your choice. Rub 2 tbsp olive oil into 6oz/175g organic oats; mix in 1 tbsp raw cane sugar and 1 tbsp sunflower seeds. Put on top of fruit and bake in a moderate oven for 15-20 minutes (until just golden).

Really quick fruit crumble

Fill an oven-proof dish with stewed fruit of your choice. Top with 150g (6oz) good quality muesli.
Dot with a few small pats of butter and bake 15-20 minutes in a moderate oven.

Sautéed apples

Peel, core and slice one apple per person and sauté in a little butter and olive oil. Drain and serve with a dollop of Greek-style yoghurt, crème fraiche or soya cream.

Chestnut cream

500g/1 lb can unsweetened chestnut puree
1 tbsp raw cane or molasses sugar
juice and (scrubbed) rind of an orange
6 tbsp Greek-style yoghurt or crème fraiche

Put the chestnut puree, sugar, orange juice and rind into a food processor or blender and blend until smooth. Add 4 tbsp of crème fraiche or yoghurt and blend again. Put into individual glasses or dishes and top with the rest of the yoghurt or crème fraiche. Top with grated nuts or chocolate.

Toffee bananas

4 bananas
2 tbsp raw cane sugar
4 tbsp orange juice

Place the peeled bananas in a shallow ovenproof dish. Sprinkle with the sugar over them and add the orange juice. Put into a medium oven, or under the grill until the sugar bubbles.

13

Satisfying Stir-Fries

One of my favourite ways of creating a high-speed meal is a stir-fry - not least because of the minimal amount of washing-up it creates. The most important advantage, however, is the amount of flavour and the high nutritional content, with the protein part of the meal taking on the flavour of the vegetables and any herbs and spices you may wish to add.

Use either a large stainless steel frying pan with a well-fitting lid, an electric frying pan or a wok.

Start by gently frying a chopped onion in 1-2 tablespoons of Extra Virgin olive oil until transparent. To this add any vegetables you may have to hand such as carrots, peppers, leeks, sweet potatoes, celery, fennel, all thinly sliced. If adding courgettes, broccoli or cabbage, I tend to add these a little later as they need a bit less cooking. If using spices, this is the time to add them, stirring while they cook a little. When all the vegetables have softened, add a little stock or a tin of chopped tomatoes for moisture. Season to taste with fresh or dried herbs, sea salt and freshly ground pepper.

At this point, there is a variety of different protein foods which can be added to make a complete meal:

1. Make a hollow, or hollows, in the vegetable mixture and break in 2-3 free range eggs per person.

2. Place one salmon steak or fillet per person to steam and absorb the flavours from the vegetables. Cook until the salmon is cooked but still moist.

3. Stir in the drained and rinsed contents of one 400g (14oz) tin for every two people of any of the following:

> Kidney, flageolet, pinto, aduki or black-eyed beans
> Chickpeas
> Lentils

4. 50g/2 oz chopped tofu, plain or marinated) per person

5. 50g /2oz quorn pieces or quorn mince (please note that, for some reason, quorn mince does contain wheat just in case you need to know this).

6. 25-50g /1-2 oz grated cheese per person

7. 50g/2 oz fresh or defrosted frozen prawns

8. 50g/2oz of the following:
    chopped almonds, hazelnuts, walnuts fresh or lightly toasted
    sunflower or pumpkin seeds, fresh or lightly toasted.

If you wish to use meat or poultry, the method is slightly different:

Put 1-2 tbsp extra virgin olive oil into a large frying pan, Add the meat (50-100g/2-4 oz per person) to seal on both sides and partially cook. Remove and set aside..

Fry a chopped onion - you may need to add a little more oil - until transparent, followed by your choice of vegetables, finely chopped.

Return the meat or poultry to the pan and simmer until all are cooked.

If you like a sauce, add some stock with 1 tbsp flour to thicken, some vegetable juice, a tin of chopped tomatoes or a little wine red - or white for poultry, red for beef, lamb or pork.

To complete the meal, serve with 50g/2oz per person of brown rice, millet or quinoa; a chunk of wholemeal bread and/or a large green salad.

Stir-fried tempeh (fermented soya)

1 small onion, chopped
4 tbsp tamari
Juice and grated rind of 1 orange
350g/12oz tempeh (from Health Food shop)
175g/6oz spring onions, chopped
225g/8oz Chinese leaves, shredded

4 tbsp sesame oil
2 tsp honey
1 tbsp grated ginger
1 tbsp olive oil
225g/8 oz mushrooms, sliced
175g/6oz beansprouts

The tempeh is best sliced and marinated overnight in a mixture of the onion, sesame seed oil, tamari, honey, orange juice and rind, ginger and garlic.

Drain the tempeh. Heat the olive oil in a wok, and stir-fry the tempeh until the edges turn brown. Move to the side of the wok and add all the prepared vegetables. Cook, stirring constantly, for 3 minutes. Mix the tempeh and vegetables together and stir in the marinade. Heat through and serve on a bed of rice.

14 Meal in a Soup

For a quick, easy and substantial lunch or supper dish, how about a Big Soup, which is a meal in itself? What's more it limits the washing up to one pot, one sharp knife and possibly a blender.

There are endless variations on the theme if you have a few basic store cupboard essentials.

> Tinned plum tomatoes
> Onions
> Carrots
> Celery
> Stock cubes or bouillon powder
> Olive oil
> Herbs dried or fresh

Most soups begin with the process of putting 1-2 tbsp olive oil into a large pan, heating it gently (NEVER over-heat oils!), adding some finely chopped onion and cooking until it becomes transparent. After that it can just be a question of adding a selection of any vegetables which you have in the fridge (or garden if you're really lucky) and cooking until they have "sweated ". At this stage add stock, or boiling water mixed with a stock cube or 1-2 heaped tsp bouillon (stock) powder, bring to the boil, and simmer until cooked.

A soup feels more like a complete meal if you also add in some form of protein. I generally do this at the end to prevent over-cooking and just before liquidizing if the soup is to be a smooth one.

Useful additions are:

> Left-over cooked chicken or meat
> Lentils
> A variety of tinned beans
> Tinned chick peas
> Sunflower seeds, ground or whole
> Tofu

Other additions might be:

> Tomato puree
> Wholegrain rice or barley
> Pasta shapes
> miso

Celeriac soup

500g/1 lb celeriac, trimmed and cubed
1 litre/1 ¾ pints milk or soya milk
50g/2 oz piece of fresh root ginger, peeled and chopped
sea salt and freshly
ground black pepper
50gr/2oz sunflower seeds

Put all the ingredients except the sunflower seeds into a large pan, bring to the boil and simmer until the celeriac is quite soft. Purée in a food processor, reheat and season to taste. Serve hot with raw or lightly toasted sunflower seeds.

Beanie soup

2 tbsp olive oil
2 medium carrots
2 - 3 cloves garlic
1-2 onions
a few sticks of celery
1 litre/1¾ pints stock
1 leek (or any other vegetables you have in the fridge)
1 x 400gram/14 oz tin of beans (or chickpeas, or lentils) drained
A generous pinch of dried herbs or a large handful of fresh herbs

Sauté chopped onion for a few minutes, then add other vegetables, chopped, and cook for a further 5-10 minutes. Add the beans, herbs if dried, and stock. Season to taste and simmer until vegetables are cooked. If using fresh herbs, finely chop and add near the end of cooking time.

From Italy

Real minestrone For four people:

1 onion
2 carrots
1 handful of shredded cabbage
I tin kidney beans
1 tin chopped plum tomatoes
fresh parsley
fresh or dried Basil
1 stock cube or 2 tsp Marigold stock powder
2 tbsp olive oil
1 clove garlic
1 litre/1 ¾ pints water
50g/2 oz pasta shapes, or broken spaghetti

Warm the olive oil over a low heat and gently cook the finely chopped onion, garlic and carrot or 2-3 minutes. Dissolve the stock cube or bouillon powder in 1 litre/1¾ pints of boiling water, or use fresh chicken or vegetable stock. Add the contents of the tins of tomatoes and kidney beans, and the stock. While it is simmering throw in a handful of chopped cabbage or other greens and the herbs. Add a sprinkling of freshly grated Parmesan cheese.

This is delicious served with olive or sun-dried tomato Ciabatta bread.

From Germany

Sausage soup

Ideal for cold winter's day, German Sausage soup follows the same method and uses basically the same ingredients. Instead of the tins of chopped tomatoes and haricot beans, add to the basic vegetable based soup, a smoked sausage ring, cut into small chunks, and either a handful of lentils, or a tin of chick peas. Any chopped root vegetable, such as parsnip of swede or turnip can be added, but be sure that you simmer long enough for them to be properly cooked.

Let the soup simmer gently for about 10 - 12 minutes to ensure that the sausage is properly heated through and the lentils are soft, but not disintegrated.

The flavour is greatly enhanced by adding half a glass of lager or light ale while the soup is simmering. and a plenty of fresh ground pepper.

Before serving add a handful of fresh chopped parsley and serve with pumpernickel or rye bread.

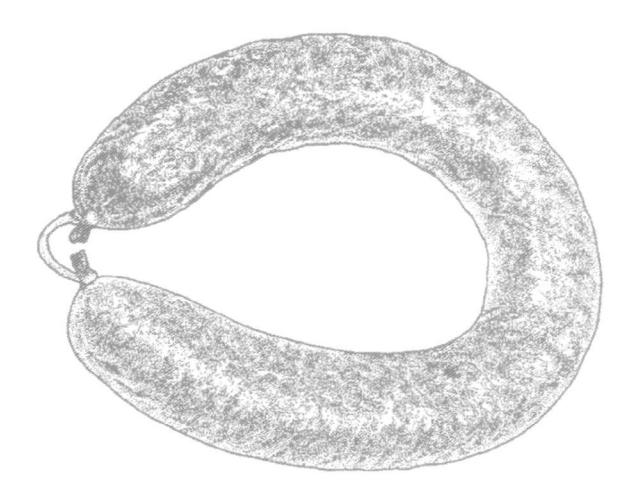

From Provence

Mediterranean fish soup

(Serves 4)

1 tablespoon olive oil	1 tin tuna in brine
1 onion	1 bay leaf
1 clove of garlic	fresh or dried basil
1 tin chopped tomatoes	thyme, rosemary, parsley as available
1 courgette	A generous glass of white wine
1 carrot	Freshly ground pepper

1lb/500g haddock, cod or coley (frozen pieces are readily available in neat squares from supermarkets).

Poach the fish in a mixture of white wine and water for about 10 minutes. When cool remove the skin and bones if any, and flake. Reserve the stock to use in the soup.

Heat the olive oil, and gently cook the chopped onion, courgette, and carrot. Add the tinned tomato, herbs, stock, wine and the flaked fish. Simmer gently for 5 to 7 minutes.

For a touch of luxury, add a few shelled prawns in the last couple of minutes, but do not over cook. For that authentic provencal flavour, serve with a spoonful of garlic rouille - available from good supermarkets - with croutons and grated cheese.

From Scotland

Scotch broth

This is a nourishing, sustaining soup, which is an excellent way of using up left-overs

The essential ingredients are onions, carrots, barley and lamb. A handful of fresh peas and some fresh chopped parley certainly add to the visual appeal of this soup.
Use one, lean, chump chop per person (or trim any visible fat) or small pieces of lamb left over from a roast.

Place barley, finely chopped carrots, onions, and any other available root vegetables, chops or pieces of lamb and about 100 grams/4 oz of barley in a large pan, and add 1 litre/1 ¾ pints of cold water. Bring to the boil and simmer slowly for at least an hour to make sure that the barley is well cooked. Add 100 grams/4 oz of frozen peas in the last five minutes of cooking and chopped parsley just before serving.

This broth can be served either with oatcakes or crusty wholemeal bread. Irish soda bread also provides a very good accompaniment.

Cockie-leekie

(Serves 4)

This is another soup with Scottish flavour. Again left-overs of chicken or beef can be used but ideally it is better to cook a couple of legs or thighs to produce a good chicken stock. The addition of a piece of stewing beef is a traditional but optional extra.

4 chicken legs or thighs
about 100g/4 oz stewing steak
2 large leeks
100g/4oz rice
1 litre/1¾ pints water
freshly ground pepper
100g/4 oz dried prunes (buy the variety which do not need pre-soaking)

Put all the ingredients in a large pot and simmer for a good 40 - 50 minutes. Remove the chicken joints & cut the meat away from the bone. Remove fat. Chop the beef & return to the pot and bring to the boil. Serve with crusty wholemeal bread or with oatcakes.

From Central America

Black bean soup (or any tinned beans)

Here is a good substantial vegetarian or vegan soup, which lends itself to the slow cooker method.

Ingredients:

1 tin of black beans (400g/14 oz) or any beans in water which you may have in the cupboard.
1 onion
1 carrot
A quarter teaspoon each of mace and cinnamon
1 small green chilli, finely chopped
For serving - slices of lemon and soured cream or crème fraiche
3 sticks of celery, a bouquet garni of mixed herbs, or dried herbs such as bay leaf, thyme, and parsley

Fry the vegetables, finely chopped, in a little olive oil, until soft. Add 1 litre/1¾ pints water; bring to the boil and simmer until tender. Add the beans, drained, and bring back to boiling. Liquidize in a blender or food processor. Serve with a spoonful of soured cream and a slice of lemon on top.

From the Far East

Hot and sour soup

This soup can incorporate either small pieces of chopped cooked chicken, meat, or tofu

100g/4oz fresh mushrooms
2 chopped spring onions
2 pieces of lemon grass, with the outer coating stripped off and then cut in large pieces
2 tablespoons sesame or olive oil
1 litre/1 ¾ pints stock
1 tablespoon dry sherry
2 tablespoons wine vinegar
1 teaspoon soy sauce
half a teaspoon Tabasco sauce
a pinch of chilli powder

100-200g/4-7 oz of tofu or chopped, cooked, chicken or meat depending on how substantial a meal you want. A blend of tofu and meats works very well.

Gently cook the sliced mushroom and spring onion in oil. Add all the other ingredients and simmer for about 10 minutes. Remove the lemon grass - it can be very chewy!

Creamy pea soup

1 tbsp Extra Virgin Olive oil
1 little gem lettuce (preferably organic)
600ml/1 pint stock (ham stock works well)
2 tbsp Greek-style organic yoghurt

4 spring onions
450g/1lb frozen peas
1 tbsp fresh mint
freshly ground black pepper

Gently heat the olive oil and add the spring onions, shredded lettuce and peas. Add the stock and gradually bring to the boil. Simmer for 5-7 minutes, add the mint, chopped, and the seasoning, and purée in a food processor or blender. Add ½ tbsp yoghurt to each dish and swirl to decorate.

Smoked haddock chowder

2 tbsp extra virgin olive oil
1 bay leaf
2 medium potatoes, scrubbed and diced
1 tbsp chives
250g/8 oz undyed smoked haddock, cubed
can of sweetcorn, drained and rinsed

1 onion, chopped
a sprig of fresh thyme
600ml/1 pint milk or soya milk
150ml/¼ pint water
freshly ground pepper 375g/12 oz
a little sea salt if required

Gently heat the oil in a medium-sized pan. Fry the onion until transparent then add the bay leaf, thyme, potato, sweetcorn, milk and water. Simmer for 10 minutes then add the fish and continue to simmer for a further 5 minutes. Season to taste and decorate with chopped chives.

Lentil soup

½ pint/275 ml Puy lentils
1 heaped tbsp miso paste
1 large onion, chopped
1 tbsp tomato purée
1½ pints/1 litre) water
¼ tsp mixed dried herbs
Seasoning to taste

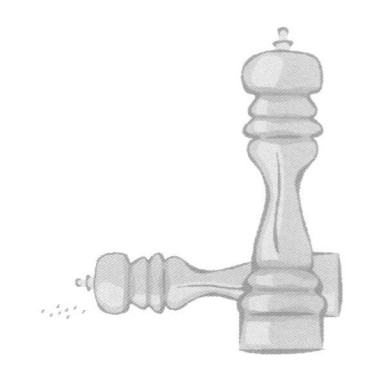

Simmer all the ingredients until cooked (about 30 minutes), Liquidize and serve with wholemeal or rye bread.

Chickpea, chilli and coriander soup

1 tin chickpeas (reserve liquid)
1 level tbsp coriander seeds
6 cloves of garlic, peeled and crushed
juice and grated rind of 1 lemon
1-2 small red chillies, deseeded and chopped

2 tbsp butter or olive oil
1 level tbsp cumin seeds
1 level tsp ground turmeric
15g/ ½ oz fresh coriander

Dry roast the coriander and cumin seeds for 2-3 minutes, then crush or grind. Melt the butter or oil in a pan, add the crushed spices together with the garlic and chillies. Cook over a low heat for about 5 minutes. Add the turmeric, stir and heat gently. Remove pan from heat.

Liquidize the chickpeas in their liquid until smooth. Add the lemon zest, chopped coriander and spices from the pan. Blend again, adding hot water to give the desired thickness. Simmer for 20 minutes and add lemon juice. Serve with crusty bread or wheat-free toast.

Snacks

Like many other people, I was brought up never to eat between meals. Often, however, eating healthy snacks throughout the day can be far more beneficial than arriving at the scheduled meal-time ravenously hungry.

The people who benefit most from "grazing", or eating little and often, fall into two main categories. They are those with:

Low blood sugar (hypoglycaemia)

There is no doubt that people with a tendency to hypoglycaemia feel better and more energetic, and think more clearly, when they eat little and often. Such snacks should preferably contain some form of protein - nuts, seeds, peanuts, beans, lentils, chickpeas, tofu or other soya product, cheese, poultry or fish - together with fruit, vegetables or other complex (unrefined) carbohydrate such as wholemeal or rye bread; Ryvita, oatcakes or rice cakes. Such foods are low on what is known as the "Glycaemic Index of Foods" and, because they are broken down slowly into glucose, the fuel for both the body and the brain, they are able to keep blood sugar levels balanced for much longer.

Although a sugary snack provides a short-term "quick-fix", achieving a rapid rise in blood sugar levels, it will not take long for those sugar levels to drop again, thus requiring another coffee or chocolate bar or cigarette. The worst time of day is often 4 o'clock when blood sugar levels are at an all-time low.

Weight Problems

Recent research has shown that if two sets of people eat exactly the same quantity and quality of food throughout the day, with one set dividing the food into three meals and the other dividing it into three meals plus three snacks, those who had the additional snacks lost weight more easily. When I put people onto a specific diet for low blood sugar problems, they are amazed at how much they are expected to eat, and even more amazed when they lose weight on the diet. It really is preferably to eat a little of the right type of food *before* getting hungry.

Suitable snack foods:

- Low sugar cereal , nut, hemp or fruit bars

    Sticks of raw vegetables with a small pot of cottage cheese or protein "dip"

    Fresh fruit with a few sunflower or pumpkin seeds, almonds, hazelnuts or almonds

    A little dried fruit with one of the above seeds or nuts

    Home-made milk or soya shakes

- Plain, live yoghurt with some crunchy muesli (beware fat and sugar content)

    Rice cakes, Ryvita or oat cakes with cottage cheese, tofu "cream cheese", hummus or nut butter

- Cheese and celery or apple

- Wholemeal scone with tofu cream

    Lightly toasted sunflower, pumpkin, hulled hemp and sesame seeds. Add 1 tbsp tamari for extra flavour.

- Fresh peanuts, lightly roasted in the oven

    Cottage cheese and pineapple

- Feta cheese and tomato

Salted almonds

100g/4 oz almonds

Sea salt to taste

2 tbsp olive oil

¼ tsp cayenne pepper (optional)

Gently fry the almonds in the oil until golden and remove from the pan. If using cayenne pepper, mix with a little salt and sprinkle over almonds.

This can also be made with hazelnuts, sunflower or pumpkin seeds.

Toasted chickpeas

1 tin chickpeas

Sea salt to taste

2 tbsp olive oil

Drain and rinse the chickpeas. Put the oil into an oven dish and add the chickpeas. Turn to coat and lightly roast in a medium oven until crisp. Salt to taste if required.

Smoked salmon on rye toast

Toast some rye bread or pumpernickel until crisp. Drizzle with olive oil and spread a layer of tofu "cream cheese". Top with smoked salmon, a squeeze of fresh lemon juice and freshly ground pepper. Eat immediately.

16 Dressing for Dinner

A good sauce or dressing really can make the difference between a boring meal and a feast and the ingredients used can be positively health-enhancing. I often make double or treble quantities as the oily dressings will keep in a refrigerator, and most of the sauces can be frozen in individual pots.

The most basic of all the dressings for salad is French Dressing. You may vary the quantities according to taste, but for a good all-round salad dressing, try the following:

Into a screw-top jar, put:

> three parts Extra Virgin olive oil (or cold-pressed sunflower or safflower oil)
> 1 part cider or wine vinegar, or fresh lemon juice

and any of the following:

> freshly pressed garlic
> fresh or dried herbs
> ½ teaspoon mustard
> ½ teaspoon honey
> sea salt
> freshly ground black pepper

Shake vigorously and serve. Make enough for several meals as this does not involve any more work.

Mayonnaise

Yes, even mayonnaise in moderate amounts can be a healthy addition to a salad and is not difficult to make:

Into a blender, place two egg yolks or one whole egg (these should be room temperature) and a pinch of sea salt. Blend until frothy and add 1 tbsp fresh lemon juice or cider /wine vinegar. Slowly drip in up to half a pint of extra-virgin olive oil depending on how thick you want the mayonnaise to be. If it becomes *too* thick, add a teaspoonful of hot water.

If you would prefer something with a less 'oily' texture, you could try:

Orange dressing

2 tbsp extra virgin olive oil

3 tbs fresh orange juice

1 clove crushed garlic

sea salt and freshly ground black pepper.

A little French mustard (optional)

Blend ingredients or put into a screw top jar and shake.

And for a dressing without any oil at all:

Sunflower dressing

1/3 cup sunflower seeds, finely ground

2 tbsp fresh lemon juice

1 cup plain, live yoghurt

1 clove garlic, crushed

1 tbsp fresh herbs, chopped

Blend until smooth; season to taste.

Putanesca sauce

1 tbsp olive oil

1-2 cloves garlic, finely chopped

tin tomatoes

1 onion, finely chopped

1 small tin anchovies

Gently fry onion and garlic until translucent; fork in anchovies; add tin of tomatoes and simmer 5 minutes. For an even stronger taste, stoned black olives may be added. This is ideal with any type of pasta.

Pineapple salsa

60g/2½ oz pineapple (fresh if possible, otherwise tinned in own juice and drained)

1 tbsp red pepper, finely chopped

1 tsp green chilli, finely chopped

1 tbsp fresh coriander, finely chopped

1 tbsp fresh mint, finely chopped

2 tbsp lime or lemon juice.

Combine all ingredients and allow to blend for 10 minutes.

Bean sauce

100g/4 oz mixed cooked beans (tinned are fine)
2 sticks celery
Sufficient stock to give required consistency
pinch of dried herbs or fresh if available
A dash of soy sauce
seasoning to taste

Purée the beans in a blender with the finely chopped celery. Put into a pan with sufficient stock to give the consistency you require. Season to taste and add the herbs. Heat through and serve with brown rice and a green or mixed salad.

Walnut sauce

100g/4oz walnut pieces (ground)
juice of a lemon
2-4 cloves garlic, crushed
sea salt and freshly ground black pepper
1 tbsp olive oil
water

Put all ingredients into liquidizer and blend until smooth. Slowly add 150ml/5fl oz water, adding more if a thinner sauce is required. Serve immediately, or blend again just before serving. Delicious with baked potatoes.

Crunchy peanut dressing

1 tbsp olive oil
2 tbsp soya sauce
juice of a lemon
1 tbsp crunchy peanut butter

Blend all ingredients; season to taste. This is delicious with a rice salad made by combining 8oz/225g cooked, wholegrain rice, chopped spring onions, fresh parsley, hazelnuts and sesame seeds.

A thinner version of this, which is served hot is:

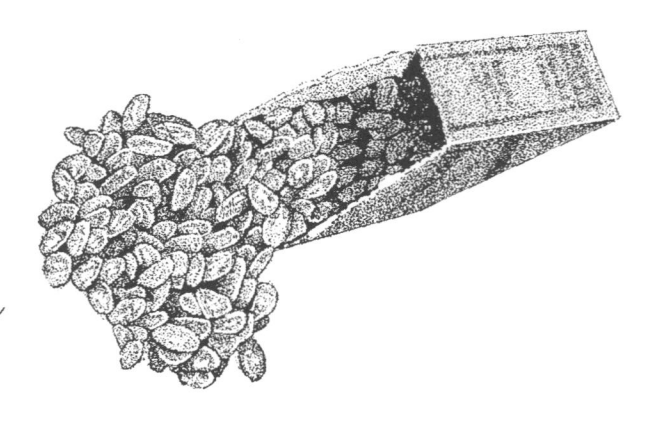

Peanut and sesame sauce

1 tablespoon peanut butter
1 tbsp tahini
1 small onion, finely chopped
200-300 ml/7-10fl oz diluted apple juice
1-2 tsp. tamari or soya sauce

Blend all ingredients together until smooth. Heat gently in a small pan, stirring constantly. The sauce will thicken as it cooks. Serve hot with any whole grain and/or vegetables.

Leek and watercress sauce

500g/1lb leeks
1 bunch watercress
300ml/10fl oz single cream
sea salt and freshly ground black pepper

1 tbsp olive oil
4 tbsp dry vermouth or white wine
450ml/ ¾ pint vegetable stock

Roughly chop the leeks and cook in olive oil 5-6 minutes until soft but not brown. Roughly chop watercress. Stir into pan with stock. Cook 3-4 minutes. Cool slightly and blend 1 minute in food processor with vermouth. Add cream and blend again until smooth.

Excellent with white fish baked in the oven.

Piquant tomato sauce

1 tbsp tomato puree
1 crushed clove garlic

300ml/½ pint plain, live yoghurt
chilli sauce or Tabasco to taste (go easy!)

Beat all ingredients together in a basin over a pan of boiling water.

This is good with chicken, turkey, lean meat. Or, you could add a tin of chickpeas; kidney, pinto, aduki, butter or flageolet beans.

Easy tomato sauce

Gently fry a chopped onion and a crushed clove of garlic in 1 tbsp olive oil until translucent. Add a tin of tomatoes and a little vegetable stock, plus some herbs (ideally fresh, but dried will do), sea salt and freshly ground black pepper to taste. Simmer for five minutes. Cool slightly and liquidize.

Really, really easy tomato sauce

For this you just need a tin of chopped tomatoes with onions. Liquidize with 1 tbsp tomato puree and required seasoning. Heat and serve.

Dressings for baked potatoes (or sweet potatoes)

Tofu dressing *see chapter 6*

Tzatziki

½ cucumber
1 clove garlic, crushed
Sea salt and freshly ground pepper to taste

1 small pot of plain, live yoghurt
1-2 tbsp fresh mint, washed and chopped

Peel the cucumber and grate into a bowl. Sprinkle with a little salt and leave for ten minutes to remove excess water. Drain and mix with the yoghurt, garlic and mint. Season to taste.

Yoghurt salad dressing

150ml/5 fl oz plain, live, yoghurt
½ tsp mustard
Sea salt and freshly ground pepper

1 tsp Tamari, or soya sauce
A little chopped parsley.
A pinch of Cayenne pepper (optional)

Stir or blend thoroughly.

If you like a stronger flavoured sauce, add 1-2 cloves crushed garlic or a generous handful of chopped chives.

Yoghurt and avocado dressing

Into the liquidizer, put the flesh of one avocado, 1 small carton plain, live yoghurt, juice of half a lime and a pinch of sea salt. Blend until smooth and creamy.

Sweet tomato dressing

Into a screw top jar or lidded container, shake together ¼ level teaspoon dry mustard, a dash of cayenne pepper, seasoning to taste, 10 tbsp Extra Virgin Olive oil, 5 tbsp cider vinegar, 2 tbsp tomato puree and a large clove of garlic, peeled. If you prefer a sweeter dressing, add a little raw cane sugar or fructose to taste. Shake well. For a mild garlic flavour, remove the clove immediately, or leave in for a stronger flavour.

Avocado dip

2 ripe avocados
1 small onion, finely chopped
1 clove garlic, crushed
150ml/5 fl oz crème fraiche
Sea salt and freshly ground pepper to taste
A dash of hot pepper sauce (optional)

Into a blender place the avocado flesh, onion, garlic and crème fraiche. Blend until smooth.

Guacamole (Mexican style)

2 large, ripe avocados
1 green chilli, finely chopped
Juice of a lime (or lemon)
Sea salt and freshly ground pepper

1 small onion, finely chopped
A few sprigs of coriander, finely chopped
4 firm tomatoes

Scrape the flesh from the avocados and mash. Add at least half the lime or lemon juice and all the other ingredients. Mix well. Add the remaining juice and eat as soon as possible.

Lemon and sesame dip *(for artichokes or chunks of raw crudities such as carrots, celery, green or red pepper etc.)*

2 tablespoons of tahini
2 tablespoons olive oil
fresh chopped parsley or coriander

juice of a lemon
freshly ground pepper

Work the lemon juice, and then the oil into the tahini. Add the pepper and fresh herbs

Sesame sauce

1 tsp arrowroot or potato flour
1 tbsp miso
1 tsp freshly grated ginger

275ml/10fl oz water
1 tsp tahini

Add a little of the water to the arrowroot. Mix well and add rest of the water. Put into a saucepan and bring to the boil. Simmer until the sauce thickens. Add the rest of the ingredients and simmer a little longer. This livens up any plain vegetables, rice or noodles.

Thai lime dressing *(this is particularly good with prawns, or with raw sliced mushrooms).*

Juice of a lime
1 tablespoon olive or peanut oil
Freshly chopped coriander leaves

½ tsp very finely chopped green chilli
1 teaspoonful light soy sauce

Put all the ingredients into a small screw topped jar and shake well to blend before using.

Green Goddess dressing

250mg/10fl oz organic crème fraiche
3 tbsp chives, finely snipped
1 clove garlic, peeled and crushed
seasoning to taste

3 tbsp parsley, finely chopped
2 tbsp anchovy paste
2 tbsp tarragon vinegar

Place all the ingredients into a blender and liquidize until smooth. This dressing is best made in advance as it thickens on standing and the flavours blend.

Tahini and orange dressing

2 tbsp tahini
2 tbsp water
1 tsp finely grated root ginger

1 tbsp olive or cold-pressed sunflower oil
juice of an orange

Mix the tahini and water, adding the water very gradually. Add all other ingredients and mix thoroughly. Good with brown rice or on salads.

Yoghurt and mustard sauce

150g/5oz plain, live yogurt
1 tbs Dijon mustard.

1 tbsp fresh parsley, finely chopped

Mix ingredients thoroughly. Excellent with grilled sardines.

Tomato and lemon salsa

500g/1lb ripe tomatoes
2 tbs chopped fresh herbs
2 tbsp fresh lemon juice
Fresh red chilli to taste de-seeded and chopped.

2-3 cloves garlic
8 tbsp extra-virgin olive oil
4-5 spring onions, finely chopped.

Mix all the ingredients together in a bowl, cover and chill for at least one hour. May be kept in the fridge for 2-3 days.

Tomato and olive sauce

2 tbsp extra-virgin olive oil
400g;14 oz can chopped tomatoes
2 tbs sun-dried tomatoes, chopped

1 red onion, chopped
3 tbs black olive tapenade
Freshly ground black pepper

Heat the oil, fry the onion until golden, then add tomatoes. Stir and heat through for a few minutes. Stir in the tapenade and the sun-dried tomatoes. Heat for 1-2 minutes and season to taste with pepper.

Excellent with chicken, pasta or fish.

The 30 Minute Dinner Party

17

An all too familiar problem for the career woman or working wife is entertaining friends or colleagues to dinner during the working week. You know that if you are very lucky you might have an hour between getting home and guests arriving. Allowing for a quick shower and change of clothes that leaves not more than 30 minutes to organise food.

Preparing dishes in advance is essential and well worth the effort. Where appropriate, they can be frozen and removed from the freezer on the morning of the party. There are, of course, some quickies which can be produced at the last moment, which do not require you to abandon your guests and disappear into the kitchen the minute they arrive, and the slow cooker, or pressure cooker, is an excellent way of cooking at least one course.

The kind of dishes which combine meat or fish, with vegetables all in one pot makes life a great deal easier. Increasingly, people are finding that they are allergic to, or intolerant of certain foods, and you may well have a request for, say, a wheat-free or dairy-free diet. Many of the recipes below fit into this category and guests who do not have such problems will really not notice any difference.

STARTERS (to serve 4 people)

Watercress soup

1 medium onion, peeled and chopped
1 medium sized cold, boiled potato
¾ pint (400 mls) water

1 tbs olive oil
1 bunch watercress, washed and chopped
2-3 teaspoons soy sauce

Gently fry the onion in the oil until transparent. Put the onion, potato, watercress and half the water into a liquidizer. Blend. Pour into a saucepan and add the rest of the water and the soy sauce. Bring to the boil and simmer 7-10 minutes. Check seasoning and serve hot or cold.

Beetroot soup

450g/1 lb fresh beetroot, trimmed, scrubbed and chopped
1 litre/1 ¾ pints stock
1 tbsp wine vinegar
150g/6 oz onion, peeled and chopped
1 small potato, chopped
1 tbsp olive oil
Sea salt and freshly ground black pepper

Gently fry the onion in the olive oil until transparent. Add the beetroot with the potato and sweat for a few minutes. Add the stock, bring to the boil and simmer until the vegetables are tender. Add the seasoning and vinegar, and liquidize. Serve with a spoonful of plain, live, yoghurt and a few snippings of chives. Very colourful!

Yoghurt and cucumber soup

1 large cucumber
2 small cartons plain, live yoghurt
1 tbsp chopped fresh dill
200ml/½ pint milk or soya milk
Pinch of paprika
sea salt and freshly ground pepper

Wash and dry the cucumber, then finely grate it. Sprinkle with salt and set aside for a short time. Rinse. Combine the cucumber with the yoghurt, herbs and seasoning and enough milk to give the right consistency. Serve chilled, topped with slices of cucumber a light sprinkling of paprika.

Mushrooms in a pot

8oz/225g button mushrooms
1 tablespoon olive oil
1 small onion, chopped
2 tablespoons tomato puree

2 tbsp red wine
1 clove garlic
Sea salt and freshly ground pepper
1 tsp parsley or mixed herbs

This can be made in advance, eaten cold or reheated. It can be made quickly at the last moment and placed in individual dishes.

Heat the oil, add the chopped onion and garlic and soften, before adding the mushrooms (cut in half if they are too big). Cook for a couple of minutes then add the rest of the ingredients and simmer gently for not more than 4-5 minutes, so the mushrooms retain their shape and texture. Serve with a scattering of chopped fresh parsley or mixed herbs.

Broccoli and goats cheese mousse

1 small goats cheese
half a packet of gelatine
2 tbsp fromage frais or Greek-style yoghurt

4 broccoli florets
fresh chives or parsley

Lightly oil four individual ramekin dishes. Then mix the gelatine in cold water in a heat proof mug. Stand the mug in the saucepan in which the broccoli is being cooked for not more than 3-4 minutes in order to dissolve the gelatine. Place the cooked broccoli, goats cheese, fromage frais, melted gelatine and fresh herbs in a food blender. Blend quickly so that there are still some pieces of broccoli visible. Spoon into the ramekin dishes and allow to set. This dish can be successfully frozen.

Melon, tomato and cucumber salad with tarragon

1 small to medium-sized honey dew melon
¼ of a cucumber
1 tbsp chopped fresh tarragon (mint, chives or parsley will fill the bill)
3 tbsp walnut oil
a few grapes or strawberries can be added

2 medium-sized tomatoes
1 finely chopped spring onion

2 tbsp cider or white wine vinegar
fresh ground pepper.

Chop the melon, cucumber and tomato into neat cubes. Place in an attractive glass bowl. Place the oil, vinegar, spring onion, pepper and chopped herbs in a small bottle or jar with a lid. Shake vigorously to blend the ingredients, then pour over the melon mixture and toss well. If making in advance, leave the herbs out until just before serving so that they keep their freshness.

Fennel and prawn cocktail

150g/6 oz fresh or frozen peeled prawns
2 tbsp olive oil
fresh parsley
a pinch of cayenne pepper

juice of a lime
1 fennel bulb
1 avocado

Carefully remove the green leafy bits from the fennel bulb and reserve for decoration. Cut the fennel into small strips, no longer than the prawns. Cut the avocado in chunks and toss in the lime juice to prevent discolouring. Shake the dressing in a jar or bottle. Mix all the ingredients together and toss in the dressing. Decorate with the green part of the fennel and with fresh parsley.

Gazpacho

450g/1 lb fresh tomatoes
1 small green pepper
1 clove garlic (crushed)
Juice of half a lemon
pepper

1 medium cucumber
2-3 spring onions or 1 small onion
a little olive oil
Sea salt and freshly ground black

Peel and chop the tomatoes, cucumber, pepper and onions into small pieces. Put into a blender with the garlic and oil until well combined. Add a little water or tomato juice if needed. Season and add the lemon juice. Serve chilled with a little diced cucumber on top.

Avocado and salmon mousse

2 ripe avocados
50-75g/2-3 oz smoked salmon pieces
juice of a lemon or lime
freshly ground pepper
5fl oz/¼ pint crème fraiche or Greek yoghurt
packet of gelatine

Dissolve the gelatine in the lemon/lime juice in a cup, over a pan of simmering water, adding a little water if necessary. Mash the avocado and mix in the finely chopped pieces of smoked salmon. Mix in the gelatine and lemon juice. Lightly whip the crème fraiche or yoghurt and fold into the mixture. Divide between four ramekin dishes and chill until set. (May be frozen). Turn out onto a bed of fresh leaves such as radiccio, rocket, lambs' leaf or frisée, lightly dressed with a walnut oil and lemon dressing.

MAIN COURSES

(serves 4 people)

Roasted salmon with mediterranean vegetables

This needs to be prepared at the very last minute.
Allow one salmon steak or fillet per person (cod or halibut work equally well).

1 red onion	4 tomatoes
1 small aubergine	2 courgettes or 1 fennel
2 tbsp olive oil	1 red pepper, deseeded
fresh herbs	

Heat the oven to 375°F/190°C/Gas Mark 5. Chop up all the vegetables. Sprinkle them generously with olive oil - and if liked, add chopped garlic - and freshly ground pepper. Place in the oven and allow to cook for about 20-30 minutes, then place the fish on top for the final 15 minutes, skin upwards, and put a little more olive oil on each. Serve on a nest of the roasted vegetables. Accompany with a mixed leaf salad with a light vinaigrette dressing or with boiled new potatoes cooked in their skins and served with a generous sprinkle of fresh chopped mint.

Plaice with cucumber

4 fillets of plaice (or 2 if very large)	2 tbsp olive oil
1 heaped tbsp wholemeal or rice flour with a pinch of sea salt	
Juice of a lemon	a cucumber, peeled and cut into chunks

Coat the plaice fillet with flour and fry in the oil, turning once (this takes about 4 minutes). Remove and put onto a warmed dish. Add the lemon juice to the pan, stir and return to the heat. Put in the cucumber chunks and heat quickly through. Arrange them on top of the fish and serve with new potatoes, green vegetables or salad.

Baked trout

4 medium-sized trout
250ml (8 fl oz) white wine
A little chopped fennel
Freshly ground black pepper

2 medium onions, chopped
4 lemon wedges
a pinch of sea salt
Sprigs of parsley

Preheat the oven to 350º C/180F/Gas Mark 4.   Rinse the trout, pat dry and put into a shallow baking dish. Sprinkle with the onions , fennel and seasoning, and pour the wine around the fish. Bake for 15-20 minutes taking care not to overcook. Garnish with lemon wedges and parsley and serve with new potatoes and some colourful vegetables.

Fish casserole

2 medium sized leeks
2 tbsp olive oil
1-1½ lbs white fish (halibut, sea bass, haddock etc.
1 tbs fresh parsley, finely chopped

1-2 red peppers (de-seeded)
4 medium sized tomatoes
¼ pint tomato juice
2 tbsp fresh lemon juice
sea salt and freshly ground pepper

Preheat oven to 350ºF/180ºC/Gas Mark 4. Wash and chop the leeks and peppers and stir-fry in the oil until tender. Add the tomato juice and the tomatoes, chopped into quarters. Season and put into a casserole dish. Cut the fish into four portions and place on top. Pour the lemon juice over the fish and sprinkle the chopped parsley on top. Cover and bake until fish is cooked (but not dry!) 15-25 minutes. Serve with new potatoes, green vegetables and/or salad.

Cooking fish in the oven is the best way to avoid fishy smells around the house.

Monkfish in tomato sauce

Tomato Sauce (see Dressing for Dinner, chapter 16)
150g/6oz Monkfish per person

Roast or steam the fish until cooked but still moist (about 20 minutes according to thickness). Serve with the tomato sauce, basmati rice and spinach, broccoli or green salad.

Liver in orange sauce

8 oz/200g lamb's or calf's liver
1 tbs olive oil
2 oranges, peeled and sliced
1 tbsp Tamari
4 tbs fresh orange juice
1 tbs wholemeal or rice flour

Cut the liver into strips, removing any stringy pieces and coat lightly in flour. Fry gently in the olive oil for 4-5 minutes. Add the orange slices, Tamari and orange juice. Heat gently and season to taste.

Curry in a hurry

Curries always taste better after being left for a few hours, so this can easily be made the night before and heated up after your guests have arrived. It will also give you time to clear the house of the aroma of curry!

3 tbsp olive oil
1 medium onion, finely chopped
1 eating apple, finely chopped
1-2 cloves garlic, crushed
1 rounded tbsp curry powder
50g/2 oz wholemeal or rice flour
50g/2 oz desiccated coconut
900ml/1½ pints vegetable stock
225g/8oz peanuts or 450g/1lb chicken or lamb cut into bite-sized pieces
A selection of vegetables, lightly cooked

Heat the oil and gently fry the onion, apple, garlic and curry powder and peanuts, chicken or lamb until the onion is soft and the meat, if using, browned. Stir in the flour, cook for 2-3 minutes, add the stock and bring to the boil. (you may prefer to use less stock for a drier curry). Simmer until thickened. Add the coconut and cook for a further 10 minutes. Cool and refrigerate.

25 minutes before you wish to eat, cook 225g/8 oz of brown basmati rice. After 15 minutes, add the vegetables to the curry and re-heat, stirring constantly.

Quick cassoulet

4 lamb chump chops

1 smoked sausage ring

2 medium sized onions

2 cloves garlic

1 tin of tomatoes

1litre/36fl oz water

mixed herbs bay leaf and rosemary if available

1 tin of haricot beans

This dish lends itself to the slow cooker method, in which case it is better to brown the chops in a little olive oil beforehand), but equally well can be cooked in advance and frozen. Either way it is easy but needs plenty of cooking time.

Chop the garlic, slice the onion. Put all the ingredients in the slow cooker or in a large ovenware casserole dish, and cook in a low oven 350°F/180°C/Gas Mark 4 for approx. 2 hours. Check from time to time that there is sufficient liquid.

This dish is good with jacket potatoes and a leafy green salad.

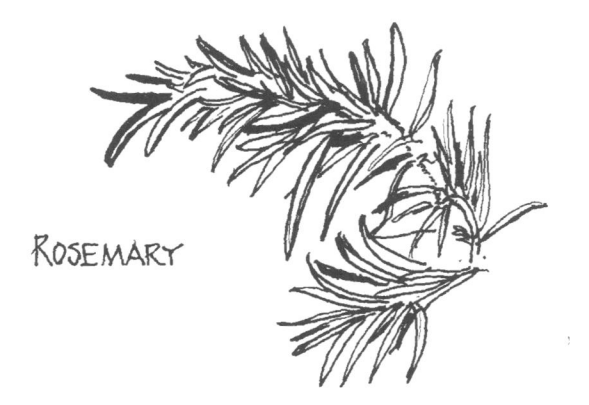

ROSEMARY

Spanish rice special

This is an adaptation of the traditional Spanish Paella. What makes it so simple is that it is all cooked in one pot, and includes rice, chicken, prawns and a selection of vegetables. It is very easy to adapt to whatever meat or vegetables are available.

- 4 chicken portions breasts or quarters
- 2 onions
- 2 oz/50g green or black olives
- 4 oz/100g fresh or frozen prawns preferably in their shells
- 4 oz/100g chorizo (Spanish style sausage) in one piece
- 8 oz/200g brown basmati rice
- a generous glass of white wine
- 2 green peppers
- 2 tomatoes
- 2 courgettes or a handful of green beans
- ½ pint/10 fl oz stock

For authentic Spanish flavour add a few strands of saffron, soaked in boiling water.

Firstly brown the chicken pieces in olive oil in a large pot. Remove. Brown the onions and peppers. Put the chicken back in the pot with the vegetables; add the rice and the chorizo sausage cut in cubes. Cover with the stock, wine, saffron and its soaking water. Bring to the boil. Turn down the heat and allow to simmer very gently for about 50 mins to an hour. Alternatively cook in a warm oven, 350°F/180°C/Gas Mark 4 for 1 hour.

So how does that fit with the 30-minute dinner party? Prepare the minute you reach home, and while you are taking a quick shower and putting the finishing touches to the table, the Paella will be gently bubbling away. Do check that it does not dry up too much and if necessary add extra liquid.

Just before serving pop the prawns on top, but do not allow to cook for more a couple of minutes.

All that is needed is a light leafy salad.

Turkey stroganoff

4 turkey escalopes (approx. 1 ½ lb/650g)
1 tbsp olive oil
8 oz/225g mushrooms
5 fl oz/150ml soured cream or crème fraiche
2 tbsp mustrd
¼ pint dry white wine and ¼ pint vegetable or chicken stock, or ½ pint stock
1 onion, finely chopped
1 tbsp flour or rice flour
1 tsp mixed herbs
1 tbsp chopped parsley
Sea salt and freshly ground black pepper

Gently heat the olive oil in a large pan and sauté the onions until transparent. Cut the escalopes into thin strips and toss in the flour. Season and add to the onions. Stir until the turkey is lightly browned. Stir in all the remaining ingredients except the cream or crème fraiche and bring to the boil. Simmer for 20 minutes; stir in the cream and gently heat. Serve with brown rice and green vegetables.

If preparing this dish in advance, do not add the cream until ready to serve. This dish can also be frozen, in which case defrost thoroughly and reheat for about 20 minutes. Add the soured cream at the last minute.

Mediterranean Vegetables

1 large aubergine
1 large bulb fennel
2 yellow peppers
8 small tomatoes
1 tsp dried basil
1 medium courgette
2 red peppers
2 small red onions
6-8 garlic cloves
1 tbsp olive oi.

Heat the oven to 425°C/220°F/Gas Mark 7. Cut the aubergine into large chunks and slice courgettes thickly. Cut fennel into quarters. Remove core and seeds from peppers. Cut into quarters. Cut tomatoes into quarters. Toss the vegetables (except tomatoes) in olive oil and basil in a large bowl. Place the contents in a baking dish. Add peeled, whole cloves of garlic and bake for 20 minutes. Add tomatoes and bake for another 10 minutes or until cooked.

PUDDINGS

(Serves 4 people)

Creole bananas

4 bananas peeled and cut in half lengthwise
50g/2 oz raw cane sugar
Juice of 2 oranges

2 tbsp rum
25g/1 oz butter

Preheat the oven to 350°F/180C/Gas Mark 4

Put the bananas into an ovenproof dish. Sprinkle with sugar and pour over rum and orange, mixed together. Dot with the butter and bake 10-15 minutes.

Cranberry and port ice-cream

The same method can be used for any strong flavoured fruit in season, for example damsons, mangoes, black currants, gooseberries or raspberries are excellent. Dried apricots or prunes are an alternative. The amount of sweetening will vary according to the sweetness of the fruit and individual taste.

250g/8 oz fresh cranberries (or other fresh fruit or dried fruit soaked overnight)
7 fl oz/200 ml water   100g unrefined cane sugar - more or less to taste.
285ml/10 fl oz double or whipping cream   grated rind of ½ an orange and ½ a lemon
2 tbsp port or appropriate liqueur alternative.
juice of ½ an orange or lemon to sharpen the flavour if required

Stew the fruit in the water and lemon juice until soft. Add sugar to taste. Liquidize and allow to cool completely. Whip the cream until firm. Fold in the fruit puree. Place in a suitable box or dish for freezing, and place in the ice box of the freezer. Once the mixture

Fruit brulée

450g/1lb stewed fruit
tbs raw cane sugar
10fl oz/½ pint Greek-style yoghurt

Put the stewed fruit into four ramekin dishes. Spoon the yoghurt over the fruit and sprinkle with sugar. Place under a hot grill until the sugar melts, but be careful not to burn. Serve immediately.

Apricot mousse with tofu

200g/8 oz dried apricots, soaked and cooked according to instructions on the packet
200g/8 oz tofu
100g/4oz Greek yoghurt, fromage frais or Yofu
Half a teaspoon ground cinnamon
2 teaspoons lemon juice
a few chopped walnuts for decoration

Cook the apricots until tender. Liquidize and cool. Blend the tofu, the yoghurt and cinnamon, then stir in the apricot puree and mix thoroughly. Spoon into individual dishes and chill well before serving, with chopped walnuts scattered on each bowl.

The same method can be used for prunes or bananas.

Lemon dream

Quick, wicked and wonderful!

500g/1 lb Greek yoghurt
350g/12oz real lemon curd (I buy mine at the local WI Market!)

Blend the yoghurt and lemon curd. Chill or can be frozen for about 5 hours. Serve with berry fruits, lightly poached with raw cane sugar and the minimum of water.
For a more "Slimline" version, use 500g low-fat yoghurt and 4 tbs lemon curd.

Chocolate mousse

8oz/225g 60% cocoa solid chocolate (Black and Greens, Lindt etc.)
3 free range egg whites
4tbs fresh orange juice or 2 tbsp orange juice and 2tbsp brandy

Grate the chocolate and melt in a bowl, with the orange juice, over a pan of hot water. Cool. If using brandy, add and mix well. Beat the egg whites into peaks and fold into the chocolate mixture. Spoon into four wine or champagne glasses and chill.

Chocolate chestnut mousse

This is one to make in advance

1 x 450g/8oz tin of chestnut purée (if using the unsweetened variety, sweeten with either 2 generous tbsp honey or 2 tbsp unrefined brown sugar
175g/6oz good quality plain chocolate
1 tbsp brandy or sherry

Melt the chocolate in a bowl over gently simmering water. Put chestnut puree and sugar, if used, in a blender and mix well with the brandy or sherry. Pour in the melted chocolate, mixing thoroughly. Spoon into individual ramekin dishes or a small bowl. Chill for at least 2-3 hours to allow the mixture to set.

For a really indulgent extra for those without special dietary requirements, top with a spoonful of whipped cream, and either a marron glacé or a sprinkle of grated chocolate.

Guava glory

Cut guavas in half (1-2 per person) and remove flesh from skin. Remove seeds and mix with a little honey. Fold into Greek-style yoghurt, fromage frais, crème fraiche or soya cream.

Strawberry and kiwi fruit

450g/1 lb fresh strawberries
4 Kiwi fruit
2 tbsp Kirsch, dry Sherry or white wine
fresh mint leaves

At least four hours before serving, slice the strawberries and the kiwi fruit and marinate in the Kirsch. Scatter a few chopped mint leaves over the fruit. Chill well before serving with Greek yoghurt or crème fraiche.

Index of recipes

almond
    apple pudding 57
    stuffed mushrooms 53
apple and cashew nut cake 36
apricot
    cream 67
    mousse with tofu 185
asparagus soup (cream of) 114
avocado
    dip 167
    paté salad 86
    and salmon mousse 176
    with smoked fish 89

bolognese sauce 100
braised
    liver and onions 101
    salmon steaks 133
braising your meat 99
bran and apple tea bread 35
bread and butter pudding 106
breakfast on the hoof 75
broccoli
    and anchovy 130
    and goat cheese mousse 174
buttermilk scones 38

calcium rich cocktail 82
cannellini bean and goat cheese salad 120
carob pudding 65

carrot
    juice 80
    and celeriac slaw 90
cashew
    hazel or almond and sunflower spread 50
    nut roast 52
celeriac soup
celery
    and almond sauce 54/129
    yoghurt and date salad 86
chestnut cream 138
chicken
    or meat broth 94
    with rice and peas 132
    and walnut casserole 54
chickpea
    chilli coriander soup 154
    and spinach curry 117
    and walnut salad 52
chocolate
    cake 35
    chestnut mousse 186
    frozen pudding 64
    mousse 186
chop supper 100
Christmas pudding 105
cleansing cocktail 81
cockie-leekie 150
coq au vin 103
cranberry and port ice cream 184

cream pea soup 153
creole bananas 184
crunchy peanut dressing 88/164
curry in a hurry 180
curried lentil soup 95

dairy (and wheat) free white sauce 27

easy tomato sauce 165
eggs florentine 133
energy breakfast 73

fennel
    and almond soup 56
    and prawn cocktail 175
fish
    casserole 178
    and corn chowder 114
    fingers 131
    provencal 97
frittata 132
fruit
    brulée
    compote with yoghurt 73
    and nut crumble 58
    and nut energy bars 41
    salad with cottage cheese dressing 86

gaspacho 176
ginger
    ale 81
    fizz 81
gram (chickpea) pancakes 38
green goddess dressing 169
guacamole (mexican style) 168
guava glory 187

hemp
    and almond pesto 51
    milk 50
hempseed
    hummus 52
    tahini 51
hot and sour soup 152
hummus 87/130

italian
    stuffed peppers 119
    style chicken breasts 102
immune booster 82

jacket potatoes 128
juicy carrot salad 51

kiwi, lime and banana frozen yoghurt 28

leek and watercress sauce 165
lemon
    curried pea soup 115
    dream 185

    and sesame dip 168
lentil
    bolognese 129
    soup 154
liver in orange sauce 179
Liz's nut roast 50
low-sugar pop 81

mayonnaise 161
meatball soup 116
mediterranean
    fish soup 148
    mackeral 127
    vegetables 183
mega muesli 74
melon
    cooler 79
    tomato & cucumber salad with tarragon 175
mixed fruit juices 79
monkfish in tomato sauce 179
mushrooms in a pot 174
monkfish in tomato sauce 179
mushrooms in a pot 174

nut
    brownies 57
    butter 48
    cream 49
    lentil paté 47/85

    milk 49
    pilaf 56

oatcakes 34
orange
    cream 68
    dressing 161

pasta
    with celery and almond sauce 33
    served with hemp pesto 127
pastry
    oat based 36
    rice based 36
pea soup 95
peanut
    butter 48
    and sesame sauce 88/164
pears in wine 104
pineapple
    juice 79
    salsa 162
    and tofutti salad 87
piperade 126
piquant tomato sauce 165
plaice with cucumber 177
poached salmon cutlets 97
porridge 74
potato cakes 38
pot roast chicken with puy lentils 119

prawn or squid provencal 134
proscuitto-wrapped leeks 116
putanesca sauce 162

quick
    cassoulet 121
    fruit crumble 137
quinoa waldorf salad 118
qourn waldorf salad 90

really
    quick fruit crumble 137
    really easy tomato sauce 166
real minestrone 146
rice
    biscuits 34
    porridge 37
    pudding 105
    salad 88
roasted
    salmon with mediterranean
    vegetables 177
    vegetables 131
rye muffins 33

salmon fingers 131
salted almonds 158
sauces and stir-fries 64
sausage soup 146
sautéed apples 138

scones 32
scotch broth 149
sesame sauce 168
smoked
    haddock 98
    haddock chowder 153
    mackeral dip 90
    salmon paté 89
    salmon with potatoes 127
    salmon on rye toast 158
soya shake 62
spanish rice special 182
spiced
    currant cookies 39
    lamb and asparagus 55
    red wine pears 120
spicy sausage with lentils 134
spinach pie 136
sprouted seed salad 55
stir-fries tempeh 142
strawberry and kiwi fruit 187
stuffed tomatoes 89
sugar-free flapjacks 42
sunflower
    dressing 162
    seed spread 48
sweet tomato dressing 167

tahini
    and orange dressing 169

spread 49
thai lime dressing 169
toasted chickpeas 158
toffee bananas 138
tofu
    blend 61
    blend 2 61
    cottage cheese 63
    creamy topping 65
    dressing 1 62
    dressing 2 66
    lemon dessert 65
    mayonnaise 62
    smoothie 73
    and spinach cannelloni 66
    tuna and anchovy dressing 64
    tuna and anchovy paté 85
Tomato
    juice 79
    and lemon salsa 170
    and olive sauce 170
    soup (creamy) 63
traditional cassoulet 99
tri-colour pepper spread 115
tuna and anchovy pasta 136
turkey stroganoff 183
tuscan tomato and basil soup 113
tzatziki 166

vegetable
    crisps 136
    soup 94
vitamin salad 87

walnut
    pavlova tart 58
    sauce 163
watercress
    soup 172
    and walnut salad 47
wheat free soda bread 31
white fish on lentils 127
winter fruit salad 103

yoghurt
    and avocado dressing 167
    and cucumber soup 173
    and mustard sauce 170
    salad dressing 166